60 Kinesthetic Grammar Activities

Other Books by Alphabet Publishing

60 Positive Activities for Adults
Teresa X. Nguyen and Nathaniel Cayanan

60 Positive Activities for Kids
Teresa X. Nguyen and Tyler Hoang

*The Drama Book:
Lesson Plans, Activities, and Scripts for the Classroom*
Alice Savage

*Successful Group Work:
13 Activities to Teach Teamwork Skills*
Patrice Palmer

50 Activities for the First Day of School
Walton Burns

*Classroom Community Builders:
Activities for the First Day & Beyond*
Walton Burns

*Keeping the Essence in Sight:
From Teaching Practice to Reflection and Back Again*
Sharon Hartle

60 Kinesthetic Grammar Activities

Alice Savage & Colin Ward
With a foreword by Scott Thornbury

Copyright Alice Savage and Colin Ward 2020

ISBN 978-1-948492-50-8 (print)
978-1-948492-51-5 (ebook)

Library of Congress Control Number: 2020903381

All rights reserved. Our authors, editors, and designers work hard to develop original, high-quality content. Please respect their efforts and their rights under copyright law.

Do not copy, photocopy, or reproduce this book or any part of this book (except for pages marked PHOTOCOPIABLE) for use inside or outside the classroom, in commercial or non-commercial settings. It is also forbidden to copy, adapt, or reuse this book or any part of this book for use on websites, blogs, or third-party lesson-sharing websites. **Discounts on class sets and bulk orders available upon inquiry.**
For permission requests, write to the publisher "ATTN: Permissions", at the address below:

Alphabet Publishing
1204 Main Street #172
Branford, CT 06405 USA

info@alphabetpublishingbooks.com
www.alphabetpublishingbooks.com

Cover photo by Val Vesa on Unsplash. "How to fold a paper fortune teller 12 steps" by Michael Phillips on Wikimedia Commons (public domain). Other illustrations by Tamsin Ward.

We are a small, independent publishing company that specializes in creative resources for teachers in the area of English Language Arts and English as a Second or Other Language. We help stock the teacher toolkit with practical, useful, and innovative materials.
Sign up for our mailing list on our website for teaching tips, updates on new books, and for discounts and giveaways you won't find anywhere else.

CONTENTS

FOREWORD · ix
ACKNOWLEDGEMENTS · xiii
INTRODUCTION · 1
TIPS FOR SUCCESS · 3
FORMATS, PROPS AND TERMS · 7
CEFR LEVELING · 9
ACTIVITIES · 13

1. *A/an* before an adjective + noun · 13
2. *A/an/some* for first mention *and the* for second mention. · 15
3. Adjectives with *too* · 18
4. Adjective clauses · 20
5. Adverbs of frequency · 21
6. Adverbs of manner · 23
7. *BE* verbs in present simple · 25
8. Comparative adjectives · 27
9. Compound Sentences with *and, but & so* · 29
10. The zero conditional with the imperative · 31
11. The 1st conditional · 32
12. The 2nd conditional · 34
13. The 3rd conditional · 36
14. The future · 39
15. The future with *will* and *won't* · 42
16. Gerunds · 43
17. Infinitives with the present simple · 45
18. Infinitives vs. gerunds · 46
19. The imperative · 49

Contents

20. Modals *can* & *can't* · 50
21. Modals *should* & *shouldn't* · 52
22. Modals past · 55
23. Nouns count & noncount · 58
24. Nouns with quantifiers · 60
25. Noun clauses · 61
26. Parts of speech · 63
27. Participial adjectives · 64
28. Participial adjectives past · 66
29. Participial adjectives present · 68
30. Passive voice · 69
31. Passive voice in the past · 71
32. Past Simple · 73
33. Past simple with yes/no questions · 75
36. Past simple and past progressive · 77
35. Past time clauses with *when* & *while* · 79
36. Past Perfect · 80
37. Phrasal verbs · 82
38. Possessive adjectives · 84
39. Prepositional phrases of time & location · 86
40. Present perfect for recent actions · 88
41. Present perfect with *ever* and *never*. · 90
42. Present perfect progressive · 91
43. Present progressive · 93
44. Present simple affirmative · 95
45. Present simple with *some* & *any* · 97
46. Present simple with negative forms · 99
47. Pronouns (subject) · 100
48. Quantifiers with food · 102
49. Restrictive and nonrestrictive clauses · 103
50. So & such · 106
51. Stative verbs · 108
52. Superlatives · 110

Contents

53. Tag questions · 112
54. *There is/There are* with prepositional phrases · 114
55. This, That, These, Those · 116
56. This, That, These, Those II · 117
57. Too & enough · 119
58. Used to · 122
59. *Wh-* questions · 123
60. Would like · 125

REFERENCES · 127

ACTIVITIES BY CEFR LEVEL · 129

ABOUT THE AUTHORS · 133

FOREWORD

THE NOTION that physical movement and gesture are implicated in language learning has a long history. As far back as the seventeenth century, the reforming educator Comenius foregrounded the use of demonstration and activity in the classroom. As Kelly (1969, p. 11) puts it, 'the Comenian classroom… was one in which both teacher and pupils were in constant activity. Teacher demonstration was followed by pupil imitation.'

In the late nineteenth century, another reformer, the Frenchman F. Gouin, was inspired by the way his young nephew recounted and re-enacted a trip to a local mill. He developed a language teaching approach in which the stages (or 'series') of a process were performed to the class, who imitated both the mime and the spoken commentary. And, a few decades later, the innovative direct method educator, Harold Palmer, promoted what he called "imperative drill" which 'consists in giving orders in the foreign language to the pupils to perform certain actions (stand up, sit down, take a book, open it, shut it, etc.)' (Palmer 1921, p.96).

The same procedure is, of course, associated with Total Physical Response (TPR), whereby imperative drill became the basis for a whole method. Its promulgator, James Asher, is quoted by Richards & Rodgers (2001, p. 73) to this effect: 'Most of the grammatical structure of the target language and hundreds of vocabulary items can be learned from the skillful use of the imperative by the instructor.' TPR aligned with other so-called humanistic teaching approaches in promoting 'whole-person' learning, where the whole person included, literally, the learners' 'heads shoulders, knees and toes'.

Nevertheless, physical activity (or kinesthetics) as a learning aid has been somewhat marginalized in recent years – restricted to the teaching of very young learners, through the use of games like "Simon says", or, in the adult language class, to the performance of role plays and simulations.

This is in part due to the prevailing view that learning – and language learning not least of all – is primarily a cognitive process. This view, in turn, dates back to the so-called 'mind-body dualism' proposed by René Descartes in the seventeenth century, and his famous adage 'I think, therefore I am.' More recently, this dualism has become further entrenched thanks to developments in the computer sciences. The mind is re-imagined as a kind of computer: Pinker (1997, p. 92), for example, describes it as 'the on-board computer of a robot made of tissue'. Hence, 'mental life can be explained in terms of a computational process' (Johnson-Laird, 1988, p.26). With regard to our own field, the 'cognitive turn' is well-captured in this claim, by Long and Richards (2001, p. vii), to the effect that 'second language acquisition is first and foremost a mental process [...] Cognition and cognitive factors, therefore, are central to any account of how and why SLA works, or so often fails.'

More recently still there has occurred what has been called an 'ecological turn' in learning theory, i.e. one that rejects the separation of mind and body and which (re)-locates language use and – by extension – language learning as being inextricably integrated into the physical and social environment. Dwight Atkinson, one of the leading proponents of this view, argues that 'cognition is a node in an ecological network comprising mind-body-world – it is part of a *relationship*' (2011: 143, emphasis in original).

This mind-body-world relationship is physically instantiated though, among other ways, movement and gesture. According to the view that cognition is embodied, gestures serve not only a communicative function, being 'co-expressive' with speech, but they also serve a self-regulatory function, by means of which

x

speakers manage their internal thought processes. Plentiful evidence suggests that gesturing while learning has important benefits: Gullberg (2008, p. 292), for example, cites studies that show that 'children who receive gestural input with vocabulary explanations retain significantly more items than those who do not. Importantly, children who also reproduce the gestures themselves perform even better than children who do not even if they have had gestural input.'

Similar effects have been found for the use of gesture in second language learning. Lindstromberg and Boers (2005), for example, demonstrated that English language learners remembered verbs better not only when they enacted them, but when they watched their classmates enact them. Such studies have led Randal Holme (2009, p. 48), among others, to argue the case for using an enactment and movement (E&M) based pedagogy, thereby 'building a bridge between movement, imagination and recollection', adding that 'the body can be rethought as the expressive instrument of the language that must be learnt' (*ibid.*) Along similar lines, the French cognitive linguist and pedagogue, Jean-Rémi Lapaire, has developed an elaborate system of teaching English grammar through mime, the core principle of which he sums up (2005, p. 3): 'Sans corps, sans matière, sans imaginaire, il n'y aurait de grammaire' ('Without body, without matter, without imagination, there would be no grammar').

This present volume continues in this exciting and innovative line, outlining a wide range of practicable activities that, in the words of the authors, 'connect language in our head to our arms and legs, eyes and ears.' They provide a welcome corrective to what the humanist educator Carl Rogers long ago termed 'education from the neck up' (quoted in Mosckowitz 1978, p. 8). Moreover, they offer an antidote to the prevailing trend in general education to take learning out of the physical space of the classroom and into the virtual space of the computer. As Claire Kramsch (2009, p. 104) observed, 'It might be that the more real-world communication takes place in the virtual world of networked computers, the more crucial it becomes for instructional environments not to emulate the computer, but to offer precisely what the computer cannot do.' What the computer cannot do is replicate that intricate meshing of language, gesture, gaze, and laughter that is inseparable from the experience of learning itself, and which brings to mind these lines of W.B. Yeats:

> *O body swayed to music, O brightening glance,*
> *How can we know the dancer from the dance?*

Scott Thornbury
The New School, New York

ACKNOWLEDGEMENTS

WE WOULD like to thank our amazing students at Lone Star College-North Harris, who are the inspiration for this book. They are the reason we wanted to make grammar learning more real by tying it to movement, experience and imagination. We are also indebted to our scolleagues at Lone Star who tried the activities with their students and offered valuable feedback in their development. We are lucky to be surrounded by dedicated professors who are willing to go off the beaten path and tap into their students' imaginations. Finally, we would like to thank our publisher and editor, Walton Burns, for taking this "leap" with us.

INTRODUCTION

The body knows things about which the mind is ignorant.
- Jacques Lecoq

OUR MINDS and bodies are in constant communication with each other and the world. Think of the butterflies you feel before public speaking, or how you can recognize confidence in your friend's posture. Often you can tell when someone is about to give you bad news simply by the sound of their voice or the look in their eyes. These are physical signs of a mental state. Even drawing can get us in touch with a part of the brain that constructs meaning.

Now imagine students sitting in rows in the classroom, their bodies still, their hands only moving pencils across the desk. How many opportunities are they missing to embody language in their voice, hands, ears, and eyes? Language is so much more than words, and that is what this book is about.

When we stand up, form a circle, get in a line according to height, frown, smile, draw a picture, use our voice to express alarm, or pretend to break an egg into a bowl, we are connecting language in our head to our arms and legs, eyes and ears. When we ask students to perform these actions, we spark curiosity, create community, and often elicit laughter. Students return to their desks energized and perhaps glad they came to class.

The activities in this book are kinesthetic insofar as they all involve some sort of physical experience which might variously be a grammar game, a role-play, a mimed scene, or even a vocal exercise. We have also included suggestions for setting up the activities with a quick review or drill, as well as variations to adjust for students at different proficiency levels. Finally, there are expansions for further practice of skills through writing and speaking activities.

Best of all, we are proud to say that the vast majority of these activities are easy to use and ready-to-go. The grammar structures are in alphabetical order for conveniently locating them when you need something on the fly, and most require little to zero prep—yes, we are working teachers! For many activities, we've included word banks and lists of cues to help get things started. Most will work in a standard classroom. Some require extra room, so don't be afraid to come up with alternative versions that take up less space.

Ultimately, we've tried to create a book that we would want to have while lesson planning, and we very much hope you enjoy using it with your students.

— *Alice & Colin*

TIPS FOR SUCCESS

BETWEEN US, we have over 50 years of experience in the language classroom, and we want to share a few things we've learned while testing these activities with different groups of learners.

1. **Expand vocabulary.** When introducing a structure, consider new vocabulary that fits with the grammar. Try some words that are not in the textbook if you are using one. For example, if you are working on past participles, your book might have *excited, interested, surprised*. Try adding some that are a little less common, for example, *impressed, annoyed, injured, beloved*, or even *spaced out*. Students may be reviewing a grammar structure they've seen before, but in this way, the activity will feel fresh, and acting out these words will add to the fun.

2. **Recognize students' state of mind.** Student energy levels can vary across a week and within a day. Some students just aren't ready to jump up and start speaking English first thing on a Monday morning. They may need a little passive input before launching into a discussion or game. On the other hand, students who are restless may have trouble following complicated sets of instructions. For this reason, you may want to stage the activity. Start by setting context, introducing vocabulary, or creating suspense with visuals. By introducing language elements first and the activity second, you are also creating cognitive connections to the aim of the lesson.

3. **Model activities.** Many of the activities require acting or using specific vocal inflections, or movements. Avoid explaining an activity to a whole class and then having to go around to each group and explain it again by carefully staging instructions

and modeling what you expect. Perform an activity yourself or partner with a strong volunteer. If students see that you are not afraid to mime riding a motorcycle or playing tennis, they will feel more comfortable doing it themselves. You can also check students' understanding by eliciting the directions back, or even by having a couple of sets of volunteers do it in front of the class prior to small group work. That way you can clarify grammar if you notice anything salient in the volunteers' performance.

4. **Attend to pronunciation.** The English sound system can influence students' sense of grammar. English speakers reduce grammar words and emphasize content words, so the phrase *I have done it* can sound like *I done it*. Not hearing the *have* in spoken English can lead students to omitting it in writing. In the statement, *I'll get a pen*, students may hear *get* and *pen*, but the schwa [ə] sound is reduced and linked to *get*, so learners may not recognize it.

Likewise, students' pronunciation challenges may affect their accuracy. For example, a student might want to say, *I enjoyed it*, but it comes out, *I enjoy it*. They have not linked *it* to *enjoyed* as a native speaker would as in *enjoy_dit*. In fact, reductions and linking in spoken English can make it hard to know where an error comes from, so identifying and highlighting missing sounds can be a great service for your students who want to speak more accurately.

5. **Consider how you want to give feedback.** Students will make errors while they are engaged in these activities. It is important to decide how you will deal with errors and correct students. Will you interrupt the activity to help the students self-correct in the moment? Or, will you take note of errors to display and discuss after the activity. There are merits to both approaches.

   In-the-moment correction: You can give a quick correction, or you can stop the activity. In the latter case, you have choices. Ask the student to rephrase or say the line up to the error and get the student to complete it. You can give hints such as "verb tense" or "word order." You can give choices, e.g. "Do you want to say excited or exciting?" This support helps the learner self-correct. When they do, or even if you supply the correction, a good rule of thumb is to have the student repeat the corrected form once or twice so the correction ends in success.

Delayed correction: Keep a list of errors you hear and write them on the board after the activity has finished. Then have students try to correct them silently before a discussion. That way, everyone can think about it, and the vocal students don't override the students who may really need the explanation. Another advantage of this technique is that it keeps the errors more anonymous.

FORMATS, PROPS AND TERMS

A FEW of these activities require a little advance preparation, and you'll need a few props: one or two balls or beanbags, drawing paper and markers, a bell, and flyswatters or rolled-up paper.

Here's a quick overview of some of the activity types and formats.

ACTIVITY	DEFINITION
An alley	Students stand in two lines face-to-face with enough space for a third student to walk down the middle.
A ball toss	Students throw a real (or virtual) ball to each other/around the room.
A chain circle	Students stand in a circle and the activity moves around the circle, one student at a time.
Cue move	Students move when they hear a specific structure.
A fishbowl	Volunteers perform an activity in front of the class.
A game, circle game	A competitive game with movement or guessing.
Hands on	Students draw or write on the board or with a pen or pencil.

60 Kinesthetic Grammar Activities

ACTIVITY	DEFINITION
An improv (improvisation)	Students take roles and act without preparation.
A line-up	Students stand in a line, sometimes in one line, and sometimes in two lines face-to-face.
Mime	Students silently act out a scenario.
A mingler	Students walk around and talk to different partners.
A role-play	Students take on roles and are given a context and time to prepare an interaction.
Sound out	Students use their voices or other sounds to communicate meaning.
A tableau	Students create a visual picture with their bodies, expressions, and gestures. They do not move.
A team game	Students form teams and take turns doing an action.

CEFR LEVELING

FOR TEACHERS who use the Common European Framework of Reference for Language (CEFR), the activities in this book have been correlated to the CEFR to indicate their intended level(s). (In the index at the back of the book, you will also find the activities categorized by CEFR level.) Most of the activities here are aimed at the beginner to high-intermediate levels (A1-B2). Many can be used in multiple levels. Variations at the end of some of the activities offer choices for leveling up an activity to meet the needs of more advanced learners. Below are descriptions for each of the six CEFR levels identifying students' abilities at the level and the grammar that is typically taught. More information about CEFR levels can be found at https://www.cambridgeenglish.org/exams-and-tests/cefr/.

A1   Basic – Beginner Level
Students are able to use very basic phrases and grammatical structures in familiar everyday expressions. They are able to maintain short, simple conversations on concrete topics and can ask and answer questions about their and other people's personal lives. Grammar taught at this level often includes structures such as the present simple, present progressive, simple past, imperatives, count nouns and basic noncount nouns, adverbs of frequency, comparative and superlative adjectives, basic modals, prepositions of time and place, subject and object pronouns, and *there is/there are*.

A2 Basic – High Beginner Level

Students are able to understand sentences and high-frequency expressions used to describe and discuss familiar topics, including personal and family information, jobs, shopping, and local geography. They are able to maintain short exchanges with others about common topics and routine events. Grammar taught at this level often includes structures from A1 with the addition of past progressive, present perfect the future with *will, be going to,* and present progressive, basic adverb clauses, common phrasal verbs, possessives, adverbial phrases, present and future modals, basic infinitives, and zero and first conditionals.

B1 Independent – Intermediate Level

Students are able to understand main ideas about topics relating to home, work, and school life, communicate about more abstract topics such as dreams and ambitions, and justify opinions with reasons. They can maintain basic exchanges with others in both familiar and less familiar contexts, and can produce short texts about themselves and topics of personal interest. Grammar taught at this level often includes structures from A1 and A2 with the addition of future progressive, present perfect progressive, noun clauses, past perfect, second and third conditionals, modals of deduction and probability, past modals, gerunds and infinitives, participial adjectives, and the passive voice.

CEFR Leveling

B2 Independent – High Intermediate Level

Students are able to understand main ideas in longer texts on both concrete and abstract topics. They can maintain exchanges with others with a high degree of fluency, produce longer texts on a wider and more complex range of subjects, and express and justify their opinions about most topics. Grammar taught at this level often includes structures from A1-B1 with the addition of future perfect, future perfect progressive, mixed conditionals, modals of speculation, adjective clauses, adverb phrases, reported speech, and conditional statements with *wish*.

C1 Proficient – Advanced Level

Students are able to understand and respond to complex texts in speaking and writing at a high level of fluency and accuracy and with great flexibility. They can communicate their opinions about social, academic, and professional topics and justify them with reasons and concrete examples in both speaking and writing. Grammar used in this level typically includes all structures, with a greater focus on using multiple genre-specific structures together for a specific, communicative purpose, for example, the use of adverb phrases and all past tenses to produce a narrative.

C2 Proficient – Mastery Level

Students are able to understand and respond to virtually all texts encountered. They can maintain long, detailed conversations about complex topics, summarize information from spoken and written texts, and express themselves fluently and precisely. They can masterfully produce all grammar structures from previous levels.

(Adapted from Council of Europe (2001a) Common European Framework of Reference for Languages: Learning, teaching, assessment, Cambridge: Cambridge University Press. https://rm.coe.int/1680459f97)

ACTIVITIES

1. *A/an* before an adjective + noun

THE GRAMMAR: *A* or *an* introduce singular nouns. Plural nouns, noun + -*s,* and noncount nouns do not need an article when used in a general sense. Articles appear before an adjective + noun and the adjective before a plural noun will not have an -*s*.
- a dangerous giraffe
- a silly cow
- a pink elephant
- cute monkeys

Aim: Students raise their awareness of article rules with adjective + noun combinations

Level: High-beginner (A2)

Preparation: A set of cues on slips of paper with an equal number of zoo animals and adjectives but an uneven number of *a/an* or -*s*. (For instance, eight nouns, 8 adjectives, 5 *a/an* and 4 – *s*)

Time: 15 – 30 minutes

Activity

1. Review the pattern of *article + adjective + singular noun*, and *adjective + noun + -s*. One way to do this is by introducing a list of animals and adjectives, that could describe them. (see the cues below for ideas). Then have pairs construct their own phrases as a practice. (You can also check students' understanding of the vocabulary words to adjust your list as necessary).

a/an	-s	dangerous	bird
a/an	-s	yellow	cow
a/an	-s	silly	elephant
a/an	camel	ugly	nervous
a/an	giraffe	angry	sleepy
a/an	snake	tiny	wild
-s	orangutan	interesting	octopus
-s	tiger	pink	monkey
-s	bear	friendly	wolf

2. Have three volunteers come up to the front and stand in a row. Give A a slip of paper with a noun, B a slip with an adjective, and C a slip with either *a/an* or *-s*. Next, tell them to move around so that they make a phrase that the class can read from left to right. They should then recite the phrase with each student saying their word, e.g., *a wild camel* or *dangerous snakes*. Don't worry if the phrases are silly. That will make them more fun and memorable. Help them with pronunciation as necessary.

   Once students understand the process, pass out the slips of paper so that each student has one of the following: *a/an* or *-s*, or an adjective, or a noun. Make sure there is an extra *-s* or *a/an* card.

3. Tell all the **nouns** to stand up and go to different parts of the room. Then tell the rest of the students to stand up, walk around, and match themselves to a noun to create a perfect singular or plural noun phrase. The goal is to move quickly and not be the odd one out!

4. When the round is up, have each group say their phrase to check. Consider adding a sentence stem such as *We saw . . .* so they can say, "We saw tiny elephants," or "We saw an ugly octopus."

(Optional) You can also have other students do a choral response, "You saw tiny elephants?" And the originals can say, "Yes, we saw tiny elephants!"

5. Have the odd one out collect all the slips and redistribute for the next round.

2. *A/an/some* for first mention *and the* for second mention.

> **THE GRAMMAR:** One feature of *a/an* is to show that there is one of something and it is being introduced to the conversation for the first time. *The* is then used to refer to the item the second time.
> - I brought some sunscreen. I put the sunscreen on my nose.
> - I found a coconut. I cracked open the coconut and drank the water inside.
> - I discovered a cave. I went inside the cave. The air was cooler than outside.

Aim: Students use *a/n* and *some* to introduce items and *the* to refer to them later

Level: High-beginner (A2)

Preparation: None. Or you can create "islands" by bunching three desks or chairs together in different parts of the room, creating "an ocean" around the room.

Time: 20-30 minutes

Activity

1. Review the patterns for articles. Give some examples such as, "I have *a* really good knife. I use *the* knife to cut open coconuts." Use the examples to point out or remind leaners that *the* is used for second mention of something.

2. Tell students they are going to sea on a ship. Then elicit or

provide a word bank of nouns on the board that can be found on a ship and an island (see below). Make sure you have examples of singular, plural, and noncount vocabulary (see below).

nouns on a ship	nouns on an island
rope	a cave
string	coconuts
wire	monkeys
blankets	a stream
a hammer	a shelter
nails	a beach
a lifeboat	rocks
matches	sand
a basket	fish

3. Tell students their ship is sinking. (You can use a picture for clarity and to get everyone "on board" with the imaginary setting.)

4. Tell them they only have time to grab five items from their ship before they fall in the water. (These can come from the word bank on the board or their own ideas.) Have them write their items on slips of paper or cards.

5. Have students stand up with their list and flounder around the room. Mime this by having them wave their arms and pretend to swim. When you clap, they should swim to an "island" formed by desks or tables.

6. On the "island," have groups share their five things with each other and discuss how they will use the items they have brought. e.g., "We'll use the rope to climb a tree." "We'll use the tools to build a shelter."

7. Give them paper to draw their island and show how they will survive.

8. Have them share their survival techniques with another group or the class, introducing the items and how they will use them to survive.

Activities

Variation

Have each group mime some of their sentences together. Have the other teams write one sentence to describe what they think it's about. When they finish, they can share their sentence. See which team was correct about the situation and note their use of articles.

Expansion

Have students write sentences about how they will use six of the items. To help students, write the frames below on the board for them to use:

- We used the ... to ...   e.g. *We used the matches to start a fire.*
- We used the ... to ...   e.g. *We climbed the coconut trees with the rope.*

3. Adjectives with *too*

THE GRAMMAR: We use *too* + an adjective to express a negative quality about a person, place, or situation. It is often followed by an infinitive to explain that an activity can't or shouldn't be done.
- I'm too angry to talk to you right now.
- He seems too young to drive.
- It's too cold to go swimming this weekend.

Aim: Students mime scenes to illustrate adjectives with *too*

Level: Intermediate (B1)

Preparation: None

Time: 15 minutes +

Activity

1. On the board, write a list of 10 adjectives with *too* and a list of 10 infinitives students are familiar with. Choose 10 each from the list below or select your own.

Adjectives	Infinitives
too big	to drive
too cold	to eat
too dark	to fall asleep
too heavy	to hold
too hot	to jump
too large	to leave
too nervous	to lift
too old	to put on
too short	to sit down
too scared	to touch
too sick	to read
too small	to ski
too tall	to talk
too tired	to walk
too young	to work

Activities

2. Review the structure by pairing adjectives with *too* and infinitives to represent a complete idea, e.g. "This bag is too big to bring on the plane." / "I feel too sick to go to work." Write example sentences on the board for reference.

3. Model the activity by selecting a phrase such as *too cold to swim*. Then mime standing at the edge of a lake, putting your toe in the water, and then shivering and shaking your head. Elicit the target phrase from students. Then have a volunteer try it to model the activity a second time.

4. Put students into pairs. Instruct each pair to secretly choose one of the adjectives and one of the infinitives and think of a scene or situation they can mime to illustrate the idea.

5. Tell the class they have 15 (or 20) seconds to guess what combination each pair is miming. Call a pair to the front of the class, set the timer, and instruct them to mime their scene. After time is up, if no one has correctly guessed the combination, ring the bell or clap to stop the activity.

6. (Optional) Give one point to the team who correctly guesses the combination first. Give two points to the pair miming the combination if it is guessed correctly.

7. Repeat steps 3 and 4 until all pairs have had a chance to mime their combinations. The pair with the most points wins.

Variation

For higher-level classes, include more academic-level adjectives, such as *careless, energetic, depressed, fatigued, frightened, immature, irresponsible, mature, serious*, etc.

4. Adjective clauses

> **THE GRAMMAR:** Adjective clauses that follow nouns start with the relative pronouns *that, when, where, who*, and *which*. They always follow the subject or object they describe. In many cases, the relative pronoun is also the subject.
> - Cars that run on electricity have enormous batteries.
> - I don't know many people who are vegetarians.
> - We saw a play which was set in the 1930s.

Aim: Students use adjective clauses to describe people they like

Level: High-intermediate - Advanced (B2-C1)

Preparation: Chairs organized into a circle with one fewer chair than the total number of students

Time: 15 minutes +

Activity

1. Quickly review adjective clauses that can describe people's looks and write them on the board for reference, e.g. *people who have brown/green/blue eyes, people who have long/short/brown/black hair, people who wear glasses*, etc.

2. Have students sit in a circle. Have one student be the "asker" and stand in the middle. Tell the asker to choose another student and ask the question: "What kind of people do you like?"

3. The student being asked must respond with *I like people who...* and complete the sentence with an adjective clause, "*I like people who...have brown eyes/like soccer/wear glasses/are single/don't eat seafood*" etc.

4. All the students who match the description must get up and sit down in an open seat. The asker and the student who gave the description must also try to find a seat.

5. The student left without a seat (odd one out) becomes the next asker, and the game continues until everyone has had a turn.

5. Adverbs of frequency

THE GRAMMAR: *Always, usually/often, sometimes, rarely/seldom, hardly ever,* and *never* tell how frequently we do things. In affirmative sentences, they are typically used before the verb. The adverb *sometimes* usually comes at the beginning or end of a sentence.
- I always drink coffee first thing in the morning.
- I usually bring a lunch. (but not always)
- Sometimes I bring a sandwich, and sometimes I bring leftovers.
- I rarely go out for lunch. (maybe once in a while with a friend)
- I never go home for lunch. (It's too far to go and come back.)

Aim: Students situate their habits in relation to others

Level: Beginner to High-beginner (A1-A2)

Preparation: A list of adverbs of frequency in big letters written on the board or large slips of paper, and a list of cues about habits (see below)

Time: 10 minutes +

Activity

1. Review with a theme such as sleep habits. Then use relevant verbs to elicit present simple sentences with routines, habits and preferences. Answer students' questions.
2. (Optional) Give volunteers a sheet of paper with one of the adverbs of frequency in large letters. Have them line up in a cline to review their relationship.
3. Post the adverbs of frequency in different places around the room or along the board. Then tell students you will say a sentence/habit. Give an example: "I bring my lunch to school."
4. Tell students to go stand next to the adverb that matches their habit. Tell them to share their habits with others and decide if

they are similar. Encourage them to make adjustments relative to each other.

5. Have them report to the group saying the sentence with their adverb to check word order.

    - I *always* bring my lunch to school.
    - I *usually* bring my lunch to school.
    - *Sometimes* I bring my lunch to school.
    - I *never* bring my lunch to school.

6. Repeat with additional sentences, having students move to that adverb of frequency, check the frequency with others, and report. You can ask how many times per week, month, or year to clarify. Here are some examples that all combine with the theme of sleep habits:

    - I stay up late on Saturday night.
    - I sleep in on Sunday morning.
    - I stay awake all night.
    - I have bad dreams.
    - I read before I go to sleep.
    - I wake up in the middle of the night.
    - I set my alarm.
    - I sleep on my side/back/stomach.
    - I take a nap.
    - I make my bed.

Expansion

Sit students in pairs or small groups. Add practice of the superlative by having them compare their sleep habits to see who is the best sleeper, the longest sleeper, the shortest sleeper, the worst sleeper, etc.

6. Adverbs of manner

THE GRAMMAR: Adverbs of manner show how people do something and typically end in *-ly*. They generally go before or after a verb. They can also go at the beginning or end of a sentence.
- She slowly raised her glass.
- He danced gracefully across the room.
- Nervously, I turned the key.
- They picked up the shovels reluctantly.

Aim: Students expand their adverb vocabulary through actions

Level: High-beginner to Intermediate (A2-B1)

Preparation: A list of adverbs and possible actions (see below)

Time: 15 minutes +

Activity

1. Review adverbs with a little game: Write a few adverbs of manner on the board, such as *slowly, nervously, courageously*. Ask students to try to figure out what kind of words these are and, if they can, add to the list. As students write new adverbs on the board, give them feedback about whether those fit the category (of adverbs) and remove or cross out those that are not adverbs. Continue adding to the list until you have 15 – 20 adverbs that can be demonstrated through miming.

angrily	forgetfully	proudly
awkwardly	gracefully	quickly
cheerfully	happily	reluctantly
courageously	hopefully	romantically
distractedly	maliciously	sorrowfully
dramatically	nervously	suspiciously
energetically	optimistically	timidly

2. Check to see that students understand the meanings. Consider demonstrating some of the adverbs through your own acting skills or those of a stronger student. Remember that students are likely to feel more comfortable dramatizing the action after they see you do it.

3. Tell students that the objective of the game is to act out the adverb silently so another person can guess it. Introduce some possible actions to get them started. Use the ones below or create your own.

walk across the room	make an omelet	drive a car
change a lightbulb	butter a piece of toast	cross a busy street
clean your glasses	peel an apple or banana	gesture to x to follow you out the door.
brush something off your pants or shirt	greet a relative	scratch your head
tie your shoes	pack a suitcase	dance
wade across a river	pick up a pen and give it to x	sweep the floor
	pet a dog	

4. Send one student (Student A) out of the room. After they leave, choose one of the adverbs to act out.

5. Invite Student A back in. Tell that student to direct a classmate to do an action. Set a timer for 2 minutes.

6. As the nominated student performs the action, A tries to guess the adverb. If they can't guess, have them nominate a second or third student to join the action/perform the action according to the adverb (alongside the first student). This continues with new students joining in and acting until the person guesses or the timer buzzes.

7. Once Student A has guessed, have a new student leave the room and repeat with a new adverb. Continue until you've reached your time limit or goal.

Variation

For a bigger class, play the game in teams. Divide the class in two. Have each side write adverbs on slips of paper to create two piles. Prepare a list of actions on the board. When it is side A's turn, the first team member comes to the front and takes a slip written by the B side. A silently acts out the adverb for their team to guess within a time limit of two minutes. If they succeed, the A team gets a point. During this time, the B side stays silent. Next, the B side takes a turn with a B student taking a slip from the A side and acting out the adverb for the B team to guess. The game continues until the slips are gone and there is a winner.

7. *BE* verbs in present simple

> **THE GRAMMAR:** We often follow *BE* verbs (*am, is are*) with adjectives and nouns to describe who people are. In questions, the *BE* verb comes before the subject, and we use a rising intonation. In short answers, we use only the subject and the verb *BE*.
> - Are you a student? → Yes, I am. / No, I'm not.
> - Is he Canadian? → Yes, he is. / No, he isn't.
> - Is she a lawyer? → Yes, she is. / No, she isn't.

Aim: Students ask and answer yes/no questions with the verb *BE* to guess famous people

Level: Beginner (A1)

Preparation: Notecards, tape, and a list of famous celebrities and historical figures

Time: 20+ minutes

Activity

1. On the board, write the names of the following categories: *Musicians / Actors / Fictional Characters / Inventors / Athletes.*

Have students work in groups to brainstorm a list of famous people for each category.

2. Elicit the students' responses and write the names on the board under the correct category or ask for student volunteers to write them down for you. Make sure all the students know them.
3. Pass out a notecard and a small piece of tape to each student. Ask each student to write the name of one of the famous people from the board. Tell students to keep their famous person a secret.
4. Instruct students to stand up and tape their notecard to another student's back without letting them see the name.
5. Have students stand up and find a partner. Instruct them to look at their partner's famous person. Then instruct each one ask and answer yes/no questions with *BE* to help them guess their secret identity. Examples might include:
    - Is she an actor? → No, she isn't.
    - Is she an athlete? → No, she isn't.
    - Is she a musician? → Yes, she is.
    - Is she alive? → Yes, she is.
    - Is she female → Yes, she is
    - Is she from the US? → No, she isn't.
    - Is she from England? → Yes, she is.
    - Is she over 60? → No, she isn't.
    - Is she blond? → Yes, she is.
    - Is she Adele? → Yes, she is!
6. Call time after 2 minute and collect the notecards. Next, have students line up and form three parallel lines. Have a student from Line A face a student from Line B. Have a student in Line C stand behind a student in Line B, also facing the student in Line A.

    Student A → ← Student B ← Student C

Activities

7. Take the notecards and stick them randomly on the backs of all students in Line B without letting them see the name.
8. Instruct students in Line A to ask questions of Student C with *BE* and *he/she* to help them guess Student B's secret identity, e.g., *Is she….?* → *Yes, she is. / No, she isn't.* Give students one minute to guess. Call time. Have students switch places again and repeat the activity so everyone has a chance to play each role.

Variation

Instead of famous people, substitute fruits and vegetables or another category of nouns.

8. Comparative adjectives

THE GRAMMAR: We add *-er* to short one- or two-syllable adjectives with that end in *-y*. We add *more* or *less* in front of longer adjectives of three or more syllables and many two-syllable adjectives without a *-y*. Sometimes we add the second item of comparison after *than*. Other times, the comparison is implied.
- Today is hotter than yesterday.
- This dress is prettier.
- A wolf is more dangerous than a dog.

Aim: Students practice making comparisons with adjectives of different syllable length as they describe pictures of people

Level: High-beginner (A2)

Preparation: A board or poster paper and markers

Time: 15-20 minutes

Activity

1. Review adjectives in regular and comparative form. Clarify that one- and two-syllable adjectives generally end in *-er*, while

60 Kinesthetic Grammar Activities

three or more syllable adjectives have *more* in front and no change. Practice a list of examples that can be used to describe people such as the following:

Smart	Strong	Short
Tall	Active	Intelligent
Lazy	Athletic	Healthy`
Old	Young	Rich
Happy	Sad	adventurous

2. Invite two volunteers to come up to the board to draw a picture. Tell A to draw a very *busy* man or woman and give the person a name. Tell B to draw a very *lazy* man or woman and give the person a name. Ask them to add as many visual details as they can. (These will often invoke laughter, which breaks the ice.)

Drawings illustrating "a tall woman" and "a short man."

Activities

3. Elicit adjectives to describe A's character depending on the details you might get, such as *smart, busy, thin, tall, nervous, stressed, rich, happy,* and *important*. (Try to elicit one-, two- and three-syllable adjectives or introduce some if you need to.) List these to the side of A's portrait.
4. Repeat with B's character. You might get *lazy, bored, poor, happy, fun, comfortable, relaxed,* and *short*. List these to the side of B's portrait.
5. Elicit a comparison from the class by asking volunteer to compare the two people in the drawings using one of the adjectives listed. Provide corrective feedback as needed.
6. Continue to invite examples, and then move on to nominating other volunteers. Add adjectives as necessary.

Variation

Have students pose according to an adjective and have class create comparisons based on the pose. For example, *Juan is more stressed than Lily.*

Expansion

Have students work in groups to write a paragraph (or a role-play) about the two people as roommates. Ask them to use at least three comparative adjectives.

9. Compound Sentences with *and, but* & *so*

THE GRAMMAR: Coordinating conjunctions include and, but, so, or, yet, for, & nor, but the most frequently occurring are and, but, & so. Coordinating conjunctions are used to combine two independent clauses (S+V), and together they make a compound sentence. Commas are used between the two independent clauses.
- I saw my friend, and she saw me.
- She saw me, but she didn't wave.
- I was confused, so I texted her.

Aim: Students work as a three-headed creature to create meaningful sentences with *and*, *but* & *so*
Level: High-beginner to Low-intermediate (A2-B1)
Preparation: None
Time: 10-20 minutes

Activity

1. Review the elements of an independent clause, and the role and meaning of the conjunctions so students understand that *and* shows an additional relationship, *but* shows contrast, and *so* shows a result. (The context of a rich boy wanting to marry a poor girl works well as a context that illustrates meaning in a broad way.)

2. Ask for three volunteers to become a "three-headed monster." When they come to the front, give them a topic such as animals or food. Then tell A to say a complete clause, tell B to say *and, but* or *so*, and tell C to come up with a new clause that shows the correct relationship of addition, contrast or result. Tell them how you plan to deal with errors. You can:
    a. Stop the activity and let them try again/give hints.
    b. Stop the activity and invite others to help.
    c. Slay the monster by replacing the person who makes the error.

3. Have the first three-headed creature create a compound sentence and give feedback on the relationships between the clauses as necessary.

4. Rotate the roles and rotate in new students so that everyone gets a turn.

10. The zero conditional with the imperative

THE GRAMMAR: The zero conditional can be used with the imperative to give instructions. The *if*-clause sets a condition for the action and can be the first or second clause of the sentence.
- Stand up if you are finished.
- Call me if you need a ride.
- If you feel tired, drink some coffee.
- If you brought food, put it on the table.

Aim: Students practice *if* clauses with the imperative
Level: High-beginner (A2)
Preparation: None
Time: 20 minutes +

Activity

1. Review the zero conditional to ensure students are aware that we can combine *if* clauses with the imperative. Write verb cues on the board and ask students to combine them with *if*.

if-clause, result clause	result clause + if-clause
have a question / ask me	make a suggestion / have an idea
want to come / text me	raise your hand / need a pencil

2. Have students sit in a circle. There should one fewer chair than the number of students. Have one student stand in the middle. Then say the first cue, "Move over if you are wearing brown shoes." Direct everyone with brown shoes to stand up. Everyone standing, including the speaker, must quickly find a new chair to avoid being the odd one out.

3. Repeat for a couple of rounds with additional cues such as "Move over if you are wearing blue" or "Move over if you like ice cream."

4. Next, have the leftover student in the center make the call, so they say, *Move over if...* Let the game continue for several rounds, making note of any need for clarification.

Variation

Introduce other forms such as past or future with the imperative such as, "Move over if you brushed your teeth this morning" or "Move over if you are going to study tonight." Note, however, that you'll have to trust them to be honest or follow through in the future.

11. The 1st conditional

> **THE GRAMMAR**: The first conditional is used to show an expected result if a condition is met. It is formed with *if* + present tense, future tense. (You can also use *may, might, can,* or *could*.) The two clauses can also be reversed, with the future clause followed by *if* + present tense.
> - If she asks me directly, I'll tell her the truth.
> - You'll need help if you want to finish on-time.
> - If you walk to school, you'll have more energy.

Aim: Students are challenged to speed up their fluency with the first conditional by making a chain story

Level: High-beginner (A2)

Preparation: A set of prompts to start a first conditional chain story

Time: 20 minutes +

Activity

1. Review the first conditional with a traditional chain story. Have students stand and get in a circle. Then start with a conditional

Activities

sentence, e.g., *If I live with my parents, I can save money.* Direct the next student to turn the main clause into an if-clause and add an element, e.g., *If I save money, I can go on a trip.*

2. Next, tell them they are going to have a competition to see which group can come up with the most correct *if* clauses.

3. Have your class stand up and form circles of 5 or 6. (You can do one big circle if you have a smaller class.) They should repeat the activity with a new prompt, e.g. "If I join the gym…" However, there are two new features. Tell them that at any point, someone can call out, "Reverse!" and the chain immediately goes the other way, or they can call out "Fire" and everyone has to leave the circle and move to a new spot. Here are some additional prompts:

   - If I move to New York, . . .
   - If I go out to eat tonight, . . .
   - If I need money, . . .
   - If I lose my phone . . .
   - If I marry an actor . . .

   You can stop the activity here or go on to the next step.

4. Create a competition. Each group will take turns standing in a line in front of the class for their round. The rules are:

   - You have two minutes to say as many conditionals as you can in a chain story, going down the line and back to the first person.
   - You get one point for every correct example. You lose two points for an incorrect example.

5. Give each group a new prompt. Tell the other groups to make a note if they hear an error. Create a tally sheet so you can calculate correct and incorrect sentences. The winner is the group with the most correct if-clauses

	Correct	Incorrect	Total
Group A			
Group B			
Group C			
Group D			

12. The 2nd conditional

THE GRAMMAR: We use *if* + past tense/ *would or could* + base form to imagine other realities in the present. The 2nd conditional is used to give indirect advice, evaluate other people's decisions and behavior, or simply make conversation about hopes, dreams or fears. Note that the order of the clauses can be reversed. Also note that in conversational grammar, *were* is used in the if-clause, not *was*.
- I would stay away from that guy if I were her.
- What would you do if you were me?
- If I had an extra day, I could edit the video.
- If he were upset, he would say something.

Aim: Students use the second conditional to share hopes, dreams, and fears

Level: Intermediate (B1)

Preparation: Slips of paper with second conditional questions (see below)

Time: 15 minutes

Activity

1. Review the 2nd conditional and have students practice the form orally until they can use it on their own. One way to do this is to show a picture of someone who is very successful and/

or down and out. Elicit forms by asking the question, "What would you do if you were this person?" Have them ask each other in open pair drills so you can give corrections.

2. Have students stand. Then give half the students (As) a slip with a question in the conditional. Use the ones below or create your own.

   - What would you do if you were blind?
   - Where would you go if you could time travel anywhere in history?
   - Who would you like to meet if you could meet any famous person?
   - What would you do if you saw a ghost?
   - What would you do if you won the lottery?
   - If you could be famous for something, what would you want to be famous for?
   - If you could live anywhere in the world, where would you live?
   - If you could be good at a sport, what sport would you pick?
   - If you could solve any problem in the world, what would it be?
   - If you could change one thing about your life, what would it be?

3. Organize a mingler. Have students walk around to music, and when the music stops, have the As pair with those students who don't have a slip (Bs) to ask their question. Give them two minutes to talk. Then stop. Have the As give their slip to the other person. Then play the music so they walk around again. Stop the music, and this time have the Bs find a partner and ask the question.

Expansion

- Walk around and note any errors or questions for a follow-up feedback session.

- Have students pick one of the prompts that they like and write about it. Note that they will tend to write sentences that are just one clause, e.g., *I would ask Kevin Kwan many questions about his childhood in Singapore.*

13. The 3rd conditional

THE GRAMMAR: We use *If* + past perfect, *would have* + past participle to imagine other realities in the past. This form is also used to show regret. Note that the order of the clauses can also be reversed.
- If Lola had set an alarm, she wouldn't have missed her first class.
- If we had had more time, we would have finished the project.
- I would have bought you a present if I had known it was your birthday.

Aim: Students use the third conditional to retell someone's story

Level: High-intermediate to Advanced (B2-C1)

Preparation: A set of prompts to start a third conditional dialogue (see below)

Time: 30 minutes +

Activity

1. Review the pattern of the third conditional and write it on the board: *If* + past perfect, *would have* + past participle. Invite volunteers to tell you what they did yesterday or this morning. Then ask what would have happened if they hadn't done it. Elicit example sentences, and write them on the board, e.g. "If I hadn't woken up on time, I would have been late to school." Correct any errors.

2. Put students into pairs. Assign each pair one of the situations below for a role-play between two friends in which someone

makes a mistake and is telling the other about it. Tell them to come up with a place and a few details about what happened.

- You forgot to turn off the stove and burned down your kitchen.
- You posted an embarrassing photo on Instagram.
- You dropped your phone in the toilet.
- You were texting and driving and hit a cat in the middle of the street.
- You picked up the wrong bag at the airport and brought it home.
- You were using your phone in class and got sent to the principal's office.

3. Give pairs 3-5 minutes to prepare their role-play. Student A will explain the situation s/he was in, and Student B will ask questions to keep the conversation going and get more details. For example:

A: You wouldn't believe what happened to me!
B: Oh yeah? What?
A: Well, I was in the kitchen. I was going to cook some eggs on the stove, so I heated up some oil in the pan. While I was waiting for the oil to heat up, I checked my email on my computer. But then, I completely forgot about the oil in the pan!
B: Oh no!
A: Yeah! Instead, I went upstairs to take a shower! I was getting out of the shower when I started to smell something strange, so I went downstairs. There was smoke everywhere, and the pan was on fire!
B: How scary! What did you do?
A: It was really hard to see, but luckily, I had a fire extinguisher in the closet, so I used it to put out the fire. The air was so smoky that I had to open all the windows and the front and back door.

B: So, what happened to your kitchen?
A: Well, everything turned black! The cabinets, the ceiling, even the chairs.
B: That's terrible!
A: Yeah, so I had to go get paint and I painted all the cabinets and the ceiling. And I washed all the chairs. It took forever to clean it all up, but now, I have a brand-new kitchen!
B: Well, I guess it wasn't all bad. I guess the lesson is not to check email while you're cooking eggs?
A: Ha-ha. Yeah, I won't ever do that again!

4. Tell the class they will be doing a tableau. Ask one of the pairs of students to come to the front of the class. Then divide the rest of the class in two teams, and have each team form a semicircle around the pair in the middle of the circle.

5. Tell the groups that they must listen to the story and prepare statements using the third conditional to make observations about what happened (referring to the pattern on the board), e.g. *If Susan hadn't checked her email, she wouldn't have*

forgotten about the pan. / If Susan hadn't left the pan on the stove, she wouldn't have set it on fire. / If Susan hadn't set her stove on fire, her cabinets wouldn't have turned black. / If Susan had been more careful, she wouldn't have had to repaint her kitchen.

6. Instruct the first pair to do their role-play. At the end, invite students from each group to make their observations using the third conditional. Give a point for each correct use of the conditional. If there is a mistake, the other group can challenge it and correct it for a point. Continue until the groups have run out of observations to make.

7. Continue Step 5 until all pairs have completed their role-plays. Add up the points for each team and declare a winner.

14. The future

> **THE GRAMMAR:** We use *will* + the base form of the verb, or *BE + going to* + the base form of the verb to describe future events. *Will* often suggests a prediction or offering and *be going to* is more often used to describe plans, but there is much overlap.
> - You will be famous.
> - I am going to sail across the ocean.
> - We will move to Australia.
> - They're going to be angry.

Aim: Students make an origami fortune teller to make prophecies for each other

Level: Beginner to High-beginner (A1-A2)

Preparation: An origami fortune teller model (see below), square paper and pens

Time: 30 minutes

Activity

1. Review the elements of the future that you want to work with. Tell students they'll be creating a fortune telling machine that they can use to predict the future.

2. Give students a piece of paper and have them fold it into a fortune teller. If possible, find instructions on how to correctly fold the paper or a video to play in class. If you do not have internet or video access in the classroom, use the instructions below:

    a. Start with a square piece of paper. 8½ x 8½ inches is typical. (You can also cut a letter-sized piece of paper into a square by folding one corner over to the other side to make a triangle. Then fold that triangle in half, cut the excess off, and unfold.)
    b. **Fold** the square paper into fourths. Then **unfold** the paper and notice the center is now clearly marked.
    c. **Fold** over the four corners so that they meet evenly into the middle.

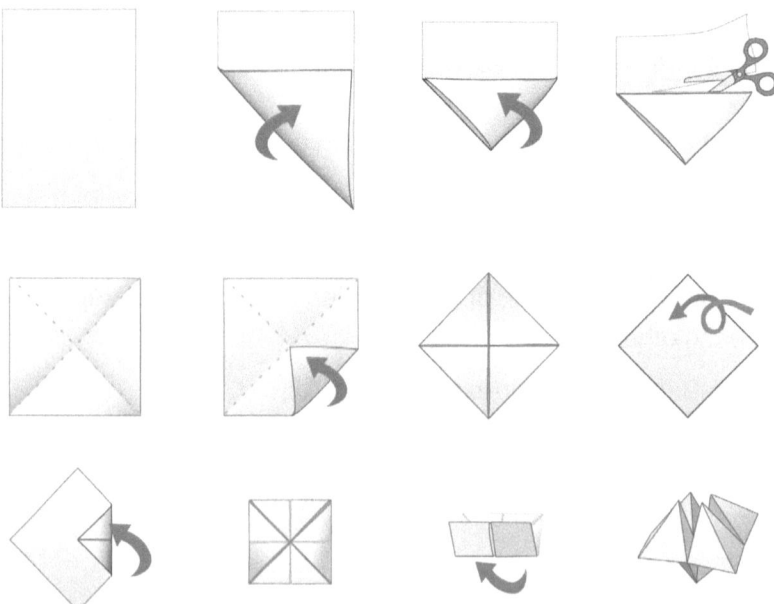

Activities

  d. **Turn over** the paper.
  e. **Fold** over the corners so they meet evenly in the middle on the new side of the paper. You now have a side with triangle flaps and a side with squares.
  f. **Fold the paper in half** so the square-side is on the outside.

3. After you've created the fortune tellers, individualize. First, instruct students to write fun words on the outside triangles, such as romance, wealth, adventure, or fame. Next, flatten out your fortune teller and unfold the inner pocket and write one sentence stem under each fold. The stem should start the prophecy. Use the examples below or create your own:
   - You will meet a stranger on a bus and…
   - You are going to do something brave but…
   - You will take a trip and…
   - You will find a magic ring, but…
   - You will get a new job and…

4. Model with a student. Put your fingers in the pockets and display it to the students. Have them pick a word from the top. Open it horizontally and say the first letter of the word, then open it vertically and say the second letter. Continue spelling the word leaving it open on the last letter. Have the student choose one of the folds. Open the fold and use the stem to start your fortune or prophecy for that student. Elaborate with three or four statements, to maximize practice, e.g. *"You will take a trip. On a tropical beach, you will meet a princess. You will save her from sharks. Her father, the king, will give you a big reward. You will buy a nice apartment in New York and have a happy life."*

5. Have students create their own fortune tellers and then take turns saying prophecies for each other. Have them move to new groups and repeat the process. You could give groups different cue words and stems to keep it interesting.

6. Have a wrap up session in which students share their favorite prophecy, e.g., *I'm going to meet a stranger on a bus. He will be a famous director. He'll ask me to be in his movie. I'll become a movie star.*

15. The future with *will* and *won't*

> **THE GRAMMAR:** We use *will* + the base form or *will not* + base form of the verb to describe future events.
> - It will rain soon.
> - You will win the race.
> - It won't happen.
> - They won't like it.

Aim: Students use *will* and *won't* to make predictions about a future event

Level: Beginner to High-beginner (A1-A2)

Preparation: Small-scale building materials such as a deck of cards, dominoes, Jenga blocks, or Cuisenaire rods, or anything that can be used to build a tower

Time: 10 minutes +

Activity

1. Review *will* and *won't* with the base form. You can do this with your rods or blocks by stacking two and then holding a third over it and asking students to predict what will happen to elicit *It will fall* or *it won't fall*. Have each student or at least several make predictions to establish that the outcome is not completely certain. If appropriate, put example language on the board.

2. Invite a volunteer to come to the front and start building a structure with the materials. Invite the other students to stand and gather round so they can see it.

3. After the student adds a new piece, ask the standing students to predict whether it *will fall* or *won't fall*. Have them stand to the left side for *will* and the right side for *won't*.

4. Then let the builder add something to the tower. The ones who predicted correctly remain standing, while the ones who didn't sit down. Then continue the pattern until the tower falls. The last student standing is the winner.

5. Repeat with a new builder.

Variation

For an easier version, complete the activity without the competition by eliciting predictions from the students who are watching.

16. Gerunds

THE GRAMMAR: A gerund is a verb + *-ing* that is used as a noun. Normally, it is treated as a noncount noun and is followed by the singular form of a verb. A gerund can be a subject, object or object of a preposition.
- Swimming makes me hungry.
- I enjoy playing Pokémon Go.
- I avoid folding the laundry if I can.
- Thank you for helping with the chores.

Aim: Students practice verbs followed by gerunds and internalize gerunds as names for actions

Level: Intermediate to High-intermediate (B1-B2)

Preparation: A list of gerunds that represent actions

Time: 10 minutes +

Activity

1. Review the role of verbs + -*ing* as nouns. Display, elicit, or pass out a list of gerunds and check that students understand the meanings.

cooking	folding laundry	sweeping the floor	gardening
walking the dog	talking on the phone	writing	painting
flying	reading	shopping	driving
dancing	watching television	playing tennis	eating

2. Model one of the gerunds as an action and show whether you like it through body language and facial expressions. Ask students to tell you what you are doing and how you feel about it. You might give them the verb *enjoy* to elicit, "You enjoy folding laundry," or "You don't enjoy driving!" Use the model to create a set of sentence frames or use the ones below.
   - You enjoy…
   - You don't mind…
   - You avoid…
   - You hate…

3. Have a volunteer come up and act out another gerund in a way that communicates their attitude. Have the other students guess using the stem. Repeat with another volunteer. Clarify that the gerund is not the verb but the object.

Expansion

Follow up with a role-play in which partner A tries to talk to partner B into doing the activity.

- *I know you don't enjoy folding the laundry, but I did it last time.*
- *Aww come on, you like walking the dog!*

17. Infinitives with the present simple

> **THE GRAMMAR:** Infinitives (*to* + verb) are often used after other verbs (e.g. *want, need, plan, etc.*). They're also used after the construction *It is* + adjective/noun phrase.
> - I want to see the Great Wall of China next year.
> - I plan to buy a house soon.
> - It is important to be prepared when you travel overseas.
> - It is a good idea to stretch before you exercise.

Aim: Students play a ball toss to practice using infinitives after verbs

Level: High-beginner to Intermediate (A2-B1)

Preparation: A ball or beanbag

Time: 10 minutes +

Activity

1. Review the form of infinitives with the present simple. One option is to ask them to use *I want to see/visit* . . . while sharing places on their "bucket list" of things to see before they die and check their form.

2. Have students stand in a circle. Show them the ball or the beanbag. Then say, "I want to go to Paris." Toss it to Student A. Tell A to state what you said, "S/he wants to go to Paris." Then have them add where they want to go. Instruct A to toss the beanbag to Student B who states A's wish only, e.g. "[Student A] wants to go to …, and I want to go to…"

   (Optional: Tell them how you will deal with errors either by interrupting or discussing them later.)

3. Repeat the activity with each student tossing the ball and repeating only the previous person's wish. (This keeps everyone engaged and active.)

4. Change the verb and context and repeat with different options such as the following:
   - I want to cook…
   - I like to learn about…
   - I hate to spend money on…

Variation

Repeat the activity with the structure *It is* + an adjective (or noun) + an infinitive for making suggestions. Start the activity and toss the ball, but this time have each person say *Yes, and…* + their own idea. Below are some examples.

Travel:
Teacher: It is important to pack socks.
A: Yes, and it is important to remember your toothbrush.
B: Yes, and it is important to bring money.

Meeting your friend's parents:
Teacher: It is good to bring flowers.
A: Yes, and it's nice to be polite.
B: Yes, and it's rude to arrive late.

18. Infinitives vs. gerunds

> **THE GRAMMAR:** Some verbs in English are followed only by gerunds (verb + *-ing*). Other verbs are followed only by infinitives (*to* + verb). A third group can be followed by either a gerund or an infinitive.
> - She wants to go hiking this weekend.
> - I can't stand waiting in long lines.
> - My dog likes swimming in the ocean, but he doesn't like to take baths.

Aim: Students practice using gerunds and infinitives through miming

Level: Intermediate to High-intermediate (B1-B2)

Preparation: A list of verbs followed by gerunds and verbs followed by infinitives (see below)

Time: 10 minutes +

Activity

1. Review the patterns of gerunds and infinitives by creating phrases or sentences with the verbs in the chart below and adding gerunds.

verbs + gerunds	verbs + infinitives
avoid, can't stand, consider, detest, discuss, dislike, enjoy, go, keep, practice, quit, recommend, suggest, understand	agree, appear, don't care, claim, decide, fail, hope, intend, plan, pretend, seem, tend, try, wait

2. Form two or three equal teams. Tell students they will be racing to mime an action and say a sentence with a verb and the correct gerund or infinitive. One student will mime the action and another will say the sentence. The first team to say a correct sentence and act it out appropriately wins.

3. Have two members of each team come to the board. Call out two verbs: a verb followed by a gerund or infinitive, and an action verb (or phrasal verb) of your choice, for example: *fail* and *lick*. A list of action verbs that are fun to act out include the following:

bite	cross out	crawl	cut up	dance
dig	dive grab	drag	fall	fly
give back	growl	hide	hug	injure
invade	jump	kick (out)	kiss	lick
march	pack	panic	party	pick up
play	pull	put on	race	repair
rip	rob	scream	shoot	shut off
sip	steal	slap	sniff	spin
spray	tear down	trap	turn	whistle

(Go over the meaning of any action verbs you will use that might be new to your students.)

4. Give the pairs time to discuss the sentence they want to act out. When they are ready, they shout, "Ready!" One student says the sentence, for example, *"He failed to lick the lollipop,"* and the other mimes the action. If the sentence uses the correct form of the verb, makes sense, and matches the action, their team receives a point. If anything is incorrect, the other team gets a chance to say and act out their sentence to steal the point.

5. Repeat the process until all students have had a chance to come to the board. The team with the most points wins.

Variation

Tailor the activity to review a specific verb tense. For example, to review the present perfect, require every sentence to include that tense, e.g. *He has failed to lick the lollipop. / She has tried to dig a hole. / I have avoided partying on Tuesdays.*

19. The imperative

> **THE GRAMMAR:** The imperative is used to give commands, warnings, and advice. It is formed with the base form of the verb (no -s, -ed, or -ing ending). The subject is *you*, but it is normally implied and not stated directly.
> - Turn right!
> - Please be on time to class.
> - Have your passports ready when you board.

Aim: Students use the imperative to help each other recreate secret images

Level: Beginner (B1)

Preparation: A small stack of drawing paper

Time: 15 minutes +

Activity:

1. Review the imperative by giving directions and having students follow them, e.g., *stand up, point to the door, etc.* and clarify form.
2. Have students sit face-to-face in pairs. One student is the Describer and sits facing the board; the other student is the Drawer and has their back to the board. Give each pair two pieces of drawing paper.
3. Tell students you will be drawing a scene on the board. Easy-to-draw scenes might include a house surrounded by trees and bushes, two stick figures sitting on a bench, a sunset in the mountains, or even an arrangement of various shapes (triangles, circles, rectangles, lines, diamonds, etc.).
4. As you start drawing the scenes on the board, the Describers explain each step to the Drawers using the imperative to help them recreate it on their papers. For example:

- Draw a long line at the bottom of the page.
- Draw a house near the center of the line.
- Give the house a door and three windows. Put one window next to the door. Put the other windows above the door.
- Add a chimney to the top of the house. Have smoke coming out of it.
- Draw a tall tree to the right of the house.
- Draw two small bushes to the left of the house.

5. When you have finished drawing the scene, ask the Drawers to bring their drawings to the front of the class and stand in a line. Have them hold up their drawings for the rest of the class to see.

6. Have the class vote on the drawing that best recreated the original drawing on the board. Students will learn that the more specific their instructions are, the closer they will be to the original.

7. Have the winning team draw the next scene on the board. Have the other pairs switch seats/roles and repeat steps 2-5.

20. Modals *can* & *can't*

> **THE GRAMMAR:** We use *can* and *can't* + the base form of the verb to talk about possibility, ability, and permission. The affirmative form, *can*, has a short, unstressed pronunciation with a "schwa" sound [kən]. The negative form, *can't*, has a longer, stressed pronunciation [kænt].
> - I can speak three languages. [kən]
> - She can meet with us next week. [kən]
> - I'm sorry, but we can't hear you. [kænt]
> - You can't park your car there. [kænt]

Aim: Students distinguish the different pronunciation of *can* and *can't*

Level: Beginner to High-beginner (A1-A2)

Preparation: Two flyswatters or other objects that can used to slap the board; 15-20 sentences that use *can* and *can't* for ability, possibility, and permission (see below)

Time: 5 minutes +

Activity

1. Review the pronunciation of *can* and *can't*. Write an example sentence for each on the board and have students repeat after you: *You can go with us. / You can't be late.*

   (Optional) You can also write "1 = can and 2 = can't" on the board, say a few sentences, and have students tell you if they heard "1" or "2." Then you can have them practice with each other.

2. Draw two boxes in the middle of the board, one above the other. Write *can* in the top box and *can't* in the bottom box.

3. Divide the class into two teams. Bring a student from each team up to the board and give each a flyswatter (or a comparable slapping object, such as a rolled-up piece of paper).

4. Tell students they must listen to the sentence you say and slap the form they hear, *can* [kən] or *can't* [kænt]. Use the example sentences below or create your own.

   - I can't hear you.
   - She can take me to the airport.
   - It can get very cold in January.
   - Our dogs can't go outside at night.
   - You can take the car if you want.
   - I can't afford a new car right now.
   - You can't stay out past midnight.
   - We can see stars from our backyard.
   - He can play video games all day long.
   - We can't find a parking spot.

- I think I can come over tomorrow.
- My hybrid can go 400 miles on one tank.
- I can't believe the semester's almost over!

5. The first student to slap the correct box first gets a point for their team. Continue until all students have had a chance to come up to the board. The team with the most points wins the game.

Variation

On the board, draw three boxes. Write *ability* in the first box, *possibility* in the second box, and *permission* in the third box. Have a member from each team come up to the board with their flyswatters (or other slapping object). Say a sentence with *can* or *can't* and have the member of each team slap the function of *can* in the sentence. If the first student to slap is incorrect, allow the other student to slap the correct box and steal the point.

21. Modals *should* & *shouldn't*

THE GRAMMAR: We use *should* and *shouldn't* + the base form of the verb to give advice. We also use it when we know something is a good idea, but we might or might not do it.
- You should call your mother.
- I shouldn't eat this cookie.
- He should ask for help.
- She shouldn't spend so much money on shoes!

Aim: Students practice using *should* to give advice when they have a dilemma
Level: High-beginner (A2)
Preparation: A set of dilemmas on slips of paper (see below)
Time: 15-20 minutes

Activities

Activity

1. Review the meaning and form of *should* + base form. You can start with a dilemma and ask for advice. "My spouse wants me to become a vegan. What should I do?" Elicit suggestions such as, "You should be a vegan because it's healthy," or "You shouldn't be a vegan because it's too hard."

2. Brainstorm a list of similar dilemmas. You can start with a few ideas, but it will be good if students think of their own. Write them in terms of requests that could elicit *should* and *shouldn't* suggestions. Use the ones below or create your own.
   - My friend wants to be my roommate.
   - My brother wants to borrow money.
   - My parents want me to study medicine.
   - My boss wants me to come in on Saturday.
   - My friends want me to take a trip this weekend.
   - My sister wants me to buy her car.
   - My neighbor wants to give me a kitten.
   - My boyfriend/girlfriend wants to get married this year.

3. Have students choose a dilemma and create details by asking and answering as many *who? when? where?* and *how?*

questions as they can. Circulate and help them develop a description of the problem.

4. Create an alley by having students stand in two lines face-to-face but leaving enough room for someone to walk through.

5. Model the activity by reviewing your problem and asking the people on the left to give you reasons to say no using *shouldn't* (Line A). Ask the people on the right to give you reasons to say yes using *should* (Line B). As you walk down the alley, listen to each person's advice and give corrections as necessary. At the end, turn and tell them what you have decided to do. Then join Line A.

6. Have the first student in Line A follow you. They describe their dilemma and then walk down the alley getting advice from both sides. At the end, they can say what they have decided and then take their place at the end of Line A. Then repeat with the first person from Line B going down the line, listening to advice, saying what they've decided and joining Line B. Repeat this process several times.

(Optional) About halfway through, have the lines switch roles, so Line A gives *should* advice, and Line B gives *shouldn't* advice. Continue until everyone has had a turn.

Variation

1. Engage students by asking them to pair-share the following question: *Is it is better to live a long life or an adventurous one?* Give students time to generate ideas and then ask them for advice, eliciting examples on the board and dealing with errors.

2. Divide the class in half. Line A comes up with advice for enjoying life and living for the moment. Line B comes with advice for being healthy and preparing for the future.

3. Have the two sides face each other with enough space in the middle for someone to walk through. Then tell them you will

walk through and listen to each person give you advice. At the end, you will choose one row to join.

4. Walk slowly down the middle so that you can hear one piece of advice from each person. At the end, join the side that has convinced you.

5. Have the first student in Line A do the same and then join a side. Then the first student in Line B follows. Alternate sides until everyone has walked down the alley.

6. Reflect on which side has the most people. Discuss what that says about the class philosophy. Optional: Have them write a paragraph about the best way to live.

22. Modals past

> **THE GRAMMAR**: We use *would, could, might* or *should + have + past participle* to speculate about what did or possibly did not happen in the past. This can include guessing, thinking of potential alternative past actions, or expressing regrets, among other things.
> - His phone might have died.
> - She could have hurt herself!
> - Should we have done something?

Aim: Students practice past models by gossiping and speculating based on someone's nonverbal body language

Level: Intermediate to High-intermediate (B1-B2)

Preparation: A list of scenarios (see below)

Time: 15-20 minutes

Activity

1. Review the form and model the activity. You can do this by choosing one of the scenarios from the list below or use your

own idea. Mime the situation, for example, finding a wallet on the street, and ask the students to guess what happened. Then say, "Are you sure?" to show that this is a guess or a speculation. Now elicit something like, "*You might have found a wallet on the street.*" Discuss the form and meaning as needed and point out the structure.

Language
- You might have found a wallet
- You could have found a phone.

Scenarios
(These can be printed on slips of paper and used as cues.)

You found a kitten on the street and are looking for the owner.	You witnessed a bank robber and now the robbers are chasing you.
You have just received a very ugly sweater as a gift, and you open it in front of the giver.	You had a party last night, and today you are tired, but you have to clean up.
The electricity has gone out and it's late at night. You need to find a way to get some light in the house, e.g., a flashlight or candles.	You were driving over the speed limit and suddenly a police officer pulls you over and gives you a ticket.
You just stepped in a mud puddle, and your shoes are dirty.	You lost your keys in the grass outside your house.
You just got an email that says you are getting a raise.	You are trying to catch a bus, but you are just a few seconds too late.

You found a package outside addressed to a family member and you are trying to figure out what it is without opening it.	Someone has just served you a nice bowl of soup, but when you taste it, you discover it has been over salted.
You see an ex-boyfriend or girlfriend and you are trying to avoid them.	You just got a paper back from the teacher and it's a bad grade.
You just stepped on a piece of broken glass.	You are enjoying a walk in the woods and suddenly you see a bear!
A person next to you on the bus is trying to start a conversation, but you don't feel comfortable.	You are walking across the parking lot, and suddenly it starts to rain.

2. Divide the class into A and B teams and have them sit together. Then player 1 from each team comes to the front. Give them the first cue to act out. They can act out individually or together for 90 seconds. Then they sit, and each team has to produce a sentence that they think best describes the scene using *might have* or *could have* correctly. Assign points.
3. Repeat with player 2 from each team and continue.

Variation

To practice *should have*, give students paper and have them draw a picture of a man who is begging on the street. Then have them create a backstory. Put the students in pairs or small groups to share their portraits and ask, "What could have happened to him?" They can speak or write sentences. Then elicit examples. Finally, have the students write monologues to perform for the class as if they were this character.

23. Nouns count & noncount

> **THE GRAMMAR:** Count nouns have both a singular and plural form, such as *an astronaut/astronauts, a restaurant/restaurants, a bookshelf/bookshelves.*
>
> Noncount nouns take singular verbs. There are several different categories of noncount nouns, including:
> - **Abstractions:** advice, honesty, intelligence, information, knowledge
> - **Foods:** beef, bread, butter, fish, toast
> - **Collective groups of items:** clothing, equipment, furniture, mail, vocabulary
> - **Liquids:** coffee, gasoline, milk, water, wine
> - **Natural events:** gravity, humidity, rain, sunshine, weather

Aim: Students recognize count and noncount nouns in speech

Level: High-beginner to Low-intermediate (A2-B1)

Preparation: A list of 12-16 nouns students have been studying in class, with an equal number of singular count and noncount nouns. Categories might include food words, weather words (see below), or your own idea.

Time: 5 minutes +

Activity

1. Review the different types of nouns. Then say a noun from the list in the grammar box above and your own ideas. Instruct students to raise the number of fingers that corresponds to the column, one finger for singular and noncount nouns, and two for plural count nouns.

2. Have the students stand in a circle. Tell them they are going to hear a list of different singular count and noncount nouns. If they hear a count noun, they should walk in a clockwise direction. If they hear a noncount noun, they should walk in a clockwise direction.

Activities

3. Have students begin walking in a clockwise direction. Start with a count noun, so students know not to stop walking, and then switch to a noncount noun, so students feel the switch of direction. Continue until you have read all of the nouns to students. To make the activity easier for students, say the plural -s on count nouns (e.g. *apples, bananas, carrots,* etc.).

Food nouns		Weather nouns	
apples	beef	rain	thunder
bananas	toast	cloud	wind
cookies	milk	thunderstorm	fog
ice cream	salt	lightning	tornado
carrots	broccoli	snow	humidity
		hurricane	raindrops

Variations

- For a large class, have students form two different circles. The two circles can participate together or one at a time, with the other group watching. If you have a second group, alternate the order of the nouns, or use a different set of nouns.
- Include nouns with both count and noncount forms (e.g. *water, chicken, cheese, tea, jam, salad, noise, space, time, glass, wood,* etc.). When you say these nouns, have students stop and sway back and forth, representing the idea that these nouns could go in either direction.

24. Nouns with quantifiers

> **THE GRAMMAR:** Quantifiers explain how much of something there is, such as *some*, *a few*, *a lot of*, and *a little*. They can come before plural count nouns and noncount nouns.
> - an onion
> - a few eggs
> - some carrots
> - some flour
> - a little rice

Aim: Help students hear expressions of quantity used with food and practice saying them

Level: High-beginner (A2)

Preparation: None

Time: 10 minutes +

Activity

1. Review the expressions of quantity with items in their kitchen or home. (At lower-levels, food is often used to introduce this structure.) Elicit a list to draw from if students need support.
2. Draw three large boxes on the board. Label one singular, one plural, and one noncount.
3. Invite a volunteer to come to the board. Tell them something you have in the refrigerator or kitchen (real or imagined). For example, say *I have an apple.* Tell the volunteer to draw the item in the appropriate box. (They should draw an apple in the singular box.)
4. Say another item, and have the volunteer draw it, e.g. *I have some eggs.* (They should draw at least two in the plural box.)
5. Have the volunteer take your place and call up another volunteer to draw. Have the first volunteer say something s/he has

in their fridge while volunteer B draws it in the appropriate box. Address any errors in the moment and make sure students get the correct sound and meaning before they sit.

Variation

Use something other than food. Talk about a different room in the house to transfer to other vocabulary. You can also elicit items to create a word bank for other contexts and discuss the way the words are used. For example, if your topic is entertainment, you might discuss *That's a laugh.* vs. *You can hear laughter.*

25. Noun clauses

> **THE GRAMMAR**: Noun clauses have a subject and a verb and can function as the subject or object of sentence. They are used mainly with *Wh- words (who, what, when, where, which, & why)* as well as *that & how*.
> - What you do is not my business.
> - He is wondering whether she is pregnant.
> - I know where you got that money.

Aim: Students analyze intentions with noun clauses through voice and body language

Level: Intermediate to High-Intermediate (B1-B2)

Preparation: None

Time: 20 minutes +

Activity

1. Review by having students underline noun clauses in example sentences. Underline the noun clauses. Use conversational language such as the following.

    I know <u>what you are doing</u>!
    I think <u>you know what I'm talking about</u>.

I wonder <u>where she went</u>.
Do you want to know <u>what I think</u>?

2. Introduce different attitudes that can be communicated through voice and body language. Have students stand in a circle. Then ask them to pose in a way that shows the attitudes below. (It helps break the ice if you pose along with them.)

enthusiastic	indignant	disappointed
upset	scared	hopeful

Have them notice the body language, facial expressions, posture, and gestures that communicate the attitude. Make a list if it helps.

3. Model the activity by saying one of the sentences (below) with one of the attitudes from the box above. For example, say "I wonder what he said," as if you are afraid that he's given away information that could get you into trouble. Then invite students to guess your attitude (scared).

4. Repeat, but this time have a volunteer do it with a different attitude and a new sentence. Have other students guess.

    - You didn't tell me (that) <u>you were going to China</u>.
    - They don't care <u>what I do</u>!
    - I (don't) know <u>where you live</u>!
    - <u>How she does it</u> is anyone's guess.
    - I wonder <u>who he's talking to</u>
    - She didn't know (that) <u>he'd been married before</u>.

5. Put students in pairs. Instruct partner A to say one of the sentences with the voice and body language of an attitude. Partner B has to guess which attitude. Then them switch.

6. Have them change partners and repeat.

7. Switch again, but this time have each pair build a dialog around the sentences by adding a line before and after (or two).

8. Have volunteers perform for the class. After each, return the focus to noun clauses and provide sentence examples/frames for analyzing the situation. Have students use the frames to describe their take on the situation.
    - He wants to know how she feels.
    - She pretends not to care what he thinks.
    - He doesn't want to say which classmate he likes better.
    - She doesn't want to admit that she's wrong.

26. Parts of speech

> **THE GRAMMAR**: Nouns are people, places and things; adjectives describe nouns; verbs show actions; and adverbs give information about the manner in which something is done.
> - **Nouns:** pirates, babies, plants, birds, a table, a ticket, a name, the moon a place
> - **Adjectives:** yellow, cold, delicious, important, dangerous, tall, easy, good
> - **Verbs:** run, eat, make, ride, take, forget, dance, push, smile, think, know, feel
> - **Adverbs:** slowly, never, carefully, badly, suddenly, fast, well, now, yesterday

Aim: Students create sentences using the different parts of speech
Level: Beginner (A1)
Preparation: A set of words that includes nouns, verbs, adjectives, and adverbs that students are likely to know
Time: 20 minutes +

Activity

1. Review parts of speech by having students identify and categorize nouns, adjectives, verbs, and adverbs. Or, have them label the words in simple sentences such as the following:

- Rats eat cheese hungrily.
- Good students study hard.
- Rich people have big houses.
- Cautious drivers watch traffic carefully.

2. Create teams of about five students. Have them stand in lines in front of the board. Draw a chart with four columns on the board. Label the charts NOUN, VERB, ADJECTIVE, and ADVERB. Give one marker or piece of chalk to the first person in each line.

3. Practice the activity. Say a word one or two times, for example, *explain*. Have the first person in each line come up and write the word in the column where they think it belongs. Review the directions if necessary. Tell them that those who wrote *explain* in the VERB column are the "winners." Assign points.

4. Have the first student give their marker to the next person in line and go to the back of the line. Repeat with a new word. (If you want to use singular nouns, it's a good idea to include the article so they are exposed to the grammatical pattern.)

5. When you have played sufficient rounds, tally the points to declare a winner. Invite the students to look at the columns and ask questions, add to the list and experiment with sentence writing.

27. Participial adjectives

THE GRAMMAR: Verbs can become adjectives with the addition of *-ed* or *-ing*. The past participle *-ed* associates with the passive voice to show the noun is the receiver of action, and it typically expresses a feeling. The present participle *-ing* suggests that the noun described is the agent or "doer" of the action.

- a frightening cat
- a boring speaker
- a burning building
- a frightened mouse
- a bored audience
- a fried fish

Activities

Aim: Students distinguish past and present participial adjectives through hand gestures

Level: Intermediate to High-intermediate (B1-B2)

Preparation: None

Time: 5-10 minutes

Activity

1. Review the difference between *-ing* participial adjectives and *-ed* participial adjectives. You can use a drawing to do this. For example, draw a monster scaring a child to elicit *a frightening monster* and *a frightened boy*. Seeing the relationship visually can help clarify the role and choice of each form.

2. Tell students you will say a phrase with either an *-ing* or *-ed* participial adjective. Tell them if they hear *-ing*, they should write with their left hand on the left side of the page. If they hear *-ed*, they should write with their right on the right side of the page. Model with two volunteers at the board so you can see which hand they use.

Left hand for *-ing*	Right hand for *-ed*
barking dog	experienced captain
burning building	broken glass
flying fish	stolen treasure
frightening storm	depressed millionaire
sailing ship	deserted island
crashing waves	frightened sailor
sinking ship	confused mermaid
embarrassing mistake	bored passengers
blowing wind	embarrassed king
shooting stars	deserted island

3. Randomly say a phrase from one side or the other. Say it in a sentence as well if you want to provide more context. Watch to see that they switch hands for the different forms.

4. Have them compare notes to make sure they got the correct form in the correct column.

5. Extend the activity by having them use the phrases to create a story to share with the class. The story construction can help them work out the right meaning.

Variation

Divide up the phrases and have each student create an illustration of a phrase to share.

28. Participial adjectives past

THE GRAMMAR Past participial adjectives are formed by using the *-ed* form of the verb as an adjective (the past participle). They are often used to describe feelings people have in response to something.
- She felt excited.
- They were amazed.
- I am surprised by his behavior.
- My cat is frightened of thunder.

Aim: Students use the correct participial adjective to describe feelings and states

Level: Low-intermediate (B1)

Preparation: None

Time: 10 minutes

Activity

1. Review by eliciting or presenting a list of adjectives that describe feelings and states of mind, or use the ones below. It's okay to mix in some regular adjectives with the past participial adjectives.

Activities

relaxed	surprised	stressed	excited	tired
frightened	nervous	happy	disgusted	peaceful
inspired	impressed	overwhelmed	rejected	sad

2. Have students tell you any patterns they see and get them to notice the *-ed* ending. Tell them that these are a special kind of adjective. They are made from verbs, but they are not verbs. Tell them we will focus on these today and delete the others. (This helps them to see the participles in the same category as *happy*, *sad*, and other adjectives).

3. Have students stand in a circle. Say one of the adjectives and have everyone show you with their expression and body language what they look like when they are *bored* or *surprised*. Encourage them to have fun with it and even exaggerate the feeling or add vocalizations. Make sure everyone does it together.

4. Repeat with additional past participle adjectives, clarifying any meaning.

5. Follow this by having students mime in pairs. Student A acts out a state and B guesses based on the body language. (You can add a short line if you want to include vocalizations, but it should carry no emotion. For example, you could have them say, "The meeting is at 3 o'clock." However, the focus should be on body language.

Expansion

Have students use a frame to write practice sentences (see below). Share and clarify how they refer back to the person's state.

I feel...	relaxed	when...
	tired	
	bored	
	excited	
	frightened	
	depressed	
	respected	

29. Participial adjectives present

THE GRAMMAR: Present participial adjectives are formed with verb + *ing*. They are used to describe nouns, which are often situations and experiences. They are easily confused with past participial adjectives (*-ed*) and so are particularly challenging to teach. Students may benefit from vivid examples.
- a terrifying encounter with a bear
- an inspiring movie
- a frightening monster

Aim: Students use present participle adjectives to describe events and experiences

Level: Low-intermediate (B1)

Preparation: None, but students will need their phones

Time: 10 minutes

Activity

1. Review participial adjectives to distinguish them from their use as verbs. This can be done by having them act out how they look when they are watching a terrifying movie. (They might hide their eyes, gasp, or scream.) Ask "What is terrifying?" to make sure they associate it with the film and not the viewer. You can repeat with the other participial adjectives on the list below or move on to step 2.

2. Elicit the names of movies from different genres and match them to participle adjectives. Your list could include the following:

exciting	boring
frightening	depressing
surprising	inspiring

3. Assign individual students to use their phones to search for movie trailers with music that reflects the participial adjectives. (Or they can use any other music app they have.)

4. Have individuals play short clips of their soundtracks for a partner or the class. The partner/class describes the music. They can say it's an exciting scene, a frightening scene etc.
5. If students have seen the movie, ask them to explain why it is inspiring, depressing, etc.

Variation

Have students find photos of places on their phones that represent the different participle adjectives. Have students show the photo to a partner to guess the adjectives they had in mind.

30. Passive voice

> **THE GRAMMAR:** The passive allows us to focus on the object of a verb by moving it to the front of a sentence. When the object is used as the subject, the BE verb is used with the past participle (-*ed*).
> - You have been hired to design the new website.
> - He was awarded a full scholarship to Princeton.
> - The driver will be blamed for the accident.
> - She is admired for her beautiful voice.

Aim: Student groups act out verbs to illustrate passive and active roles
Level: High-Intermediate (B2)
Preparation: A list of verbs that can be agents and recipients (see below)
Time: 10-15 minutes

Activity

1. Review the passive voice by providing a few examples of passive and active sentences. Have students label which is which and explain what makes a sentence passive.

- Some aliens captured my brother.
- The building was destroyed in a fire.
- The ship was destroyed by a sea monster.
- A snake ate my homework.
- Alice chased a rabbit.

2. Elicit or introduce vocabulary for nouns that can be both agents and passive recipients of an action (see below). The following can help you get started. If you want to teach different tenses, you may want to identify the specific tense you want them to use such as present, past, or present perfect.

hunter/hunted	admirer/admired	forgiver/forgiven
leader/led	conqueror/conquered	photographer/photographed

3. Divide the class in half. The first half will be observers. Divide the second half into two again so you have ¼ As and ¼ Bs. Give the As the role of the hunted. Give the Bs the role of being the hunters. (Don't give observers roles.) Give the As and Bs a few seconds to think about what they will do to act out their role.

4. Clear some space in the room. Have the actors stand in different random places to take up the whole room. Tell them that when you clap, they must enact their role. Tell the observers that they will have to guess who are the hunters and who are the hunted.

5. Clap so that the actors move around the room with the hunters "hunting" the hunted. Let them do this for up to two minutes. They should have some fun with this.

6. Clap again, have them stop, and then have the observers group the students by directing them to the hunter side of the room or the hunted side of the room. Then check to see if they are right.

7. Elicit sentences using the passive voice to clarify, and have students write them if you wish.

8. Play another round. Have the actors sit and become observers. Have the observers stand, divide into As and Bs, and enact the next pair of words from the box above. (They may need a little time to create context, but it should be mostly improvised.) Continue with other transitive verbs as needed along with any follow-up clarification.

Variation

Put students in groups and have them construct a story around the context.

31. Passive voice in the past

> **THE GRAMMAR:** The passive allows us to focus on the object of a verb by moving the object to the front of a sentence. In the past tense, the passive is formed with *was/were* + past participle (*-ed*).
> - He was charged with drunk driving.
> - The trees were blown down by the storm.
> - He was kicked by a horse.

Aim: Students act out a crime scene to explore choices about active and passive voice

Level: High-intermediate (B2)

Preparation: None

Time: 30 minutes (10 min per round)

Activity

1. Review the simple past passive and active constructions and check students, understanding of criminal justice verbs that are transitive.

arrest/arrested	break/broken	charge/charged	chase/chased
catch/caught	free/freed	handcuff/handcuffed	kidnap/kidnapped
kill/killed	rob/robbed	shoot/shot	steal/stolen

2. Create three groups of students. Explain that the groups will rotate roles. Give each group a different scenario for acting out a crime story silently. Use the examples below or create your own. If you create your own, you'll have to modify the directions slightly. Instruct each group to work out the details, choose roles, and practice. Give them five or more minutes to practice.

   - **Group A: A robbery:** Some robbers break into a jewelry store and steal some diamonds. The police arrive at the scene and catch all but one of the thieves. The thief hides the diamonds.
   - **Group B: Attempted murder:** A wife puts poison in her husband's food, and he falls over at dinner table. Someone calls an ambulance. It rushes the patient to the hospital. The police arrive to investigate and arrest the wife.
   - **Group C: A kidnapping:** A gang stops a driver, ties him/her up and puts the victim in the back seat. Then they try to drive away. The police arrive and chase the carjackers. Eventually they catch, arrest and handcuff the criminals. Then they free the victim.

3. Have Group A present their mime while the others watch. Tell group B to work together to write three sentences that focus on what happens to the diamonds. Tell group C to write three sentences that focus on what happens to the robbers. They can write sentences in the passive and the active. Follow up with a discussion on how the passive helps control the focus of the text.

4. Elicit the sentences to the board, placing them in passive or active columns. Discuss the possible reasons why passive voice is a good or bad choice for the clarity of the sentence and the story. (You can also use the context to play around with different choices.)

5. Have Group B present their mime. Tell group C to focus on telling the story of the wife. Have group A focus on telling the story of the husband. Again, elicit sentences to passive and active columns and discuss. How does the passive strengthen or weaken clarity?

6. Have C present their mime. Have group A focus on writing sentences about the victim. Have group B focus on writing sentences about the carjackers. Elicit sentences to passive and active columns and discuss. Consider adding some sentences about the police, which should naturally be active since they have the most agency in the story.

Expansion

Have the groups write the story of their pantomime in sentence form. Tell them that they should use both active and passive sentences. They'll want to think about which one makes each sentence flow best.

32. Past Simple

> **THE GRAMMAR:** The past simple is used to talk about events that took place at a specific time in the past. It is commonly used to narrate actions and events that happened in sequence, such as what happened first, second, third, and so on. Past tense verbs may be regular (-*ed*) or irregular.
> - It rained all night.
> - I moved to China three years ago.
> - After the marathon, the runners were exhausted.
> - Yesterday, I had a salad for dinner.

Aim: Students create a collective story using past tense verbs

Level: High-Beginner to Intermediate (A2-B1)

Preparation: The first line of a story that can be added to (see below)

Time: 10-15 minutes

Activity

1. Review the past tense forms by eliciting as many regular and irregular past tense verbs as you can. You can do this by having students stand in a circle. Start by saying a past tense verb and pointing to a student who says a second past tense verb and then points to a third student. Continue the pattern until you've heard about 20 or 30 verbs. The only rule is that they cannot repeat a verb.

2. Have the students stand up and form two lines facing each other. Tell one line they are the *fortunately* line, and they must always say, "Fortunately" and then add a happy past tense detail. Tell the other side they are the *unfortunately* line, and they must always start by saying, "Unfortunately" and add a sad past tense detail.

3. Tell them you will start the story by throwing a ball to one of the lines. The first student to get the ball must continue the story, and then throw the ball to someone in the other line. To keep it lively, make the ball a "hot potato." Tell them it is so hot they can't hold it long so they must speak as quickly as they can and toss it to the other line.

    Use the story cues below or create your own.
    - One night, I saw a little puppy on the side of the road.
    - As I walked through the city, I realized I was lost.
    - Our bags were packed, and we were heading to the airport.
    - Nobody noticed, but while we were unpacking the car, a raccoon got into the house.

4. Start the story and toss the ball to the first student. Direct them to continue the story as quickly as possible before tossing it back to the other side. For example:

> Teacher: One night, I saw a little puppy on the side of the road.
> A: Fortunately, there were no cars.
> B: Unfortunately, it was dark, and I couldn't see very well.
> A: Fortunately, I had my phone and turned on my flashlight.
> B: Unfortunately, I didn't have much battery left.

5. Continue until all students have had the chance to add a detail to the story or until the story comes to a logical end.

Variations

- For a larger class, have students form a circle with three sections: a "Fortunately" line, an "Unfortunately" line, and a "Suddenly" line. Students in the "Suddenly" line will add a new or surprising action (good or bad) using the past simple.
- At the end of the activity, have students write the story they created as a paragraph to review the use of past tense verbs. Have lower-level students work in pairs to recreate the story.
- Link the story to one that you have recently read in class. Review the story and the common verbs used to tell the story. Write the verbs on the board for students to reference during the activity.

33. Past simple with yes/no questions

THE GRAMMAR: Yes/no questions in the past can be formed with the BE verbs *was/were* + subject + adjective or noun. They can also be formed with *Did* + *subject* + *the base form* of the verb.
- Did you go to the beach?
- Were you a quiet child?
- Was your house in the country?

Aim: Students ask questions to find out more about their classmates' childhood personalities

Level: Beginner (A1)

Preparation: None

Time: 20 minutes +

1. Review the meaning and use of yes/no questions in the past. Students should understand *was/were* + adjectives and basic regular and irregular verbs for describing childhood activities.

2. Have students write four sentences on a blank piece of paper. They should not write their names. The first sentence should have an adjective that describes them as a child, such as *curious, social, adventurous, happy, quiet,* or *serious*. The next three should tell about things the person did in their childhood such as *rode my bike, played with dolls, visited my friends, studied hard, etc*. Walk around and check for correct forms.

3. Collect the papers and then randomly redistribute them so everyone has a new set of questions. Make sure they do not have their own. Tell them to turn the sentences into questions and write them below.

4. Have everyone stand, walk around the room, and ask questions to try and find the writer of the paper. When they find that person, they can continue to chat or let someone else find them. Note: there will probably be some overlap. If someone asks them about something they didn't write even though it's true, direct students to say "Yes, but that's not me!"

Expansion

Have students tell about their partner to the class to provide more opportunities to practice.

36. Past simple and past progressive

THE GRAMMAR: The past simple (-*ed*) is used for the past actions that are in a sequence, one happening after the other. The past progressive (*was/were* + *-ing*) is used to give background information about actions and events that were in progress before and during the main actions.
- We decided to go out to eat because we didn't have much food at home.
- I was waiting for the bus and my legs were starting to hurt.
- We went to the park to play soccer. It was raining a little, so we got wet.

Aim: Students listen for the past simple and past progressive

Level: High-Beginner to Intermediate (A2-B1)

Preparation: A story with examples of the past simple and past progressive

Time: 10 minutes +

Activity

1. Review the simple past and past progressive. Read a couple of example sentences (below) in which you hop forward with each past simple verb, and glide backward with each past progressive verb. The gliding should represent a long, graceful movement backward.

    - I moved to Bellevue in 2010 (*hop*). While I was living (*glide*) there, I met (*hop*) a strange little woman.

2. Clear the room so you have plenty of space. Have students make two lines facing each other: a "past simple" line, and a "past progressive" line. Instruct them to keep 2-3 feet of distance between the lines. For larger classes, make two sets of lines facing each other.

3. Tell the "past simple" line to hop forward toward the other line when they hear a verb in the past simple. Tell the "past progressive" line to glide backward away from the other line when they hear a verb in the past progressive.

4. Read a story to the students with the simple past. Use the story below. Alternatively, create your own or use one from a textbook the students are studying from.

Farmer John had a tough weekend. On Saturday, he went to check on his cows. The cows were sitting down in the fields. A big storm was coming, and dark clouds were rolling in. Farmer John knew immediately that trouble was coming, so he decided to take action. He called to his trusty farm dog, Rusty. Rusty was sleeping in the barn, but when he heard the call, he ran straight to his owner. Rusty barked and barked. He circled the cows until they started walking toward the barn. The rain was starting to fall, and the winds were blowing, but finally, all the cows made it back to the barn safely. As the storm passed, Farmer John petted his trusty companion, Rusty, and told him he loved him.

Expansion

Have students work in pairs to create their own short story using the past simple and past progressive. Then repeat steps 2 and 3, with each pair reading their story together to the rest of the class. Have students switch lines between the stories so they have the experience of being both the "past simple" and "past progressive" line.

35. Past time clauses with *when* & *while*

THE GRAMMAR: Past time clauses show time relationships between two or more events. *When* is usually used with the simple past to show that one action happened after another action. *While* is typically used with the past progressive to explain an action that was in progress before or during another action. Past time clauses can be the first or second clause of a sentence.
- When I went to London, I visited my old friend from school.
- I gave her a big hug when I met her at the train station.
- While we were having lunch, I told her about my life and my family.

Aim: Students practice using past time clauses with the past simple and past progressive to develop and perform a story

Level: High-Beginner to Intermediate (A2-B1)

Preparation: A list of sentence cues (see below)

Time: 20-30 minutes

1. Write sentence cues on the board for a short story and have pairs discuss which to combine with *when* and which to combine with *while*. Elicit the students' ideas and write the example sentences on the board.
   - camp/have an adventure
     - While I was camping, I had an adventure.
   - look for firewood/hear a noise
     - While I was looking for firewood, I heard a noise.
   - look up/see a bear
     - When I looked up, I saw a bear.

2. Put students in small groups of 2-4 students. Give them cues (see below) and have them develop a simple story they can act out silently. Other groups must watch and then retell the story using *when* and *while*.

- You were on a bus. The driver suddenly collapsed.
- You were watching a sports game. Suddenly someone on the other team broke the rules.
- You were at the zoo. An animal escaped from its cage.
- You were at a restaurant. You saw a celebrity.
- You were at a store. A robber came in.
- You were at a park. You helped a lost child.

36. Past Perfect

> **THE GRAMMAR:** The past perfect is formed with *had (not)* + the past participle (*-ed*). It is used to explain something that happened and was finished before another past event.
> - I had forgotten my swimsuit, so I couldn't go in the water.
> - They moved slowly down the rope into the cave. It got darker and darker. The temperature dropped, but they kept going until their feet hit solid ground. They had reached the bottom.

Aim: Students become familiar with past perfect in spoken conversation

Level: Intermediate to High-Intermediate (B1-B2)

Preparation: A paragraph or two with examples of the past perfect and past tense (see below)

Time: 10 minutes +

Activity

1. Review the function of the past perfect in moving back in time. Model the activity by reading a couple of sentences in which you take a step forward with each past tense, and a step backward with each past perfect tense. Use the text below or come up with your own.

Activities

- I baked a pie and brought it to the party. I felt proud of it. I had thought people would love it, but then I noticed that no one was eating it. I took a taste and realized that I had forgotten to add the sugar!

Have students notice the way the simple past sequences forward while the past perfect sequences backward.

2. Have students stand. They should be arranged so that they have room to take steps forward and backward. Tell them to take a step forward when they hear past and a step back when they hear past perfect. Then read your text slowly and clearly enough for them to be able to identify the sound. Watch as they step. (Often, they will watch each other for clues.) Use the example text below or create your own.

When I <u>arrived</u> at college, I was so scared that I <u>changed</u> my mind. I <u>told</u> my parents I <u>wanted</u> to go home with them. My mother <u>said</u> no, they <u>had already paid</u> my tuition, and I was going, whether I <u>liked</u> it or not. Then she and my father <u>got</u> in the car and left. It was only later that I <u>found out</u> that my mother <u>had cried</u> all the way home.

Expansion

- Have students work in pairs to try and recreate the story in written form. Tell them that they must include at least two instances of the past perfect. Then have them share their results with another pair. Show the text on the board or screen and let them check. Discuss the way the past perfect makes sense in showing a reverse in the direction of time.
- Have a volunteer stand in a line and say something that happened to them when they were young. Say "step", and every time you say step, have that student tell the next thing that happened. Periodically say backstep instead. The student then needs to take a step back and use the past perfect to explain a detail in their story. (This requires a bit of modeling, but it can be fun.)

37. Phrasal verbs

> **THE GRAMMAR:** Phrasal verbs consist of a verb + a particle. A phrasal verb has a different meaning than the verb by itself. With separable phrasal verbs, object pronouns are placed between the verb and the particle. With inseparable phrasal verbs, the object pronoun is placed after the particle.
> - When he <u>asked her out</u> on a date, she said yes. (separable)
> - I got my jacket and <u>put it on</u> before we left. (separable)
> - We got our tests back and <u>went over them</u> with the teacher. (inseparable)
> - She's a lot like her father. She <u>takes after him</u> in many ways. (inseparable)

Aim: Students recognize the difference between separable and inseparable phrasal verbs

Level: High-beginner to Intermediate (A2-B1)

Preparation: 100 blank note cards for classes with around 20 students; a list of separable and inseparable phrasal verbs students have studied (see below)

Time: 10 minutes +

Activity

1. Put students in groups of three. Give each group an equal stack of 10 blank note cards and two markers. Ask each group to make two pronoun cards, writing **IT** on one notecard and **THEM** on a second note card.

2. Say a phrasal verb and *singular* (it) or *plural* (them), e.g. *take out, singular*. Students write the verb (*take*) and the particle (*out*) on separate note cards as fast as they can. Then the three students each take a card - the verb card, the particle card, and the correct pronoun card – and stand up in the correct order, e.g. *take it out*. Once all groups are standing with their

Activities

cards read, tell them to shout out the phrase, count to three and have them shout out the complete phrase, e.g. "Take it out!" Groups with the correct order get a point.

Separable phrasal verbs		Inseparable phrasal verbs	
ask out, bring about, bring up, call off, cheer up, drop off, figure out, fill in, give back	look up, make up, put back, put off, put on, show off, shut off, think over, throw away,	check into, come across, get on, get over, get through, go over	look after, look into, run into, run across, take after, take up

3. Repeat the process with singular and plural pronouns and other separable and inseparable phrasal verbs. The groups with the most points win.

Variations

- To review gender-specific pronouns, have students use and create cards for the pronouns HER and HIM instead of IT and THEM. In this case, you would say, *take out, feminine* to elicit *take her out*, or *look after, masculine* to elicit *look after him*.
- Have groups create a sentence using the phrasal verb and the pronoun for an extra point. Require that the pronoun refer back to something specific, e.g. *The garbage was smelly, so I had to take it out. / My friend was sad, so I cheered her up by telling a joke.*

38. Possessive adjectives

> **THE GRAMMAR:** Possessive adjectives (*my, your, his, her, our,* & *their*) show ownership of an item or concept. They come before nouns.
> - That was my idea!
> - She's lost her mind!
> - You forgot your keys.
> - That's his problem.
> - We need their truck.
> - This is our house.

Aim: Students practice possessive adjectives by using voice emphasis to claim ownership of an idea or item or to defer it to someone else

Level: Beginner to High-beginner (A1-B2)

Preparation: None

Time: 10+ minutes for each part

Activity

1. Review the forms of possessive adjectives by having students fill in a chart or asking questions.

2. Introduce the activity with a mini pronunciation lesson on stress emphasis. Demonstrate how we lengthen the vowel sound in words that we want to stress. In this exercise, we are stressing the possessive adjective to clarify ownership.

3. Do a choral drill by pointing to student A, tossing a ball, and saying, "Is this your ball?" Guide student A to catch it, and then use word stress to say, "No, it's not **MY** ball. It's **HER** ball." Student A should toss it to student B who repeats the phrase, saying, It's not **MY** ball. It's **HIS** ball. Continue until everyone has practiced.

4. Move on to a dialog. Write the dialog below on the board or create your own, and practice. Have students practice in A/B

turns. (Encourage them to overemphasize the word stress. Attending to their voice aids both meaning and memory.)

> A: This is *myyy* car.
> B: No, this isn't *youuuur* car. This is *ooour* car.
> A: No, I'm sorry. This can't be *youuur* car. I'm quite sure it's *myyy* car.
> B: No, no, no, you are mistaken. This is definitely *ooour* car!

5. Practice again, but this time have students practice gestures. Also have them think about how they feel. Are they upset or confused? How can they show it in the way they use their voice?
6. Practice again, and have students substitute other words for *car*, such as *dog, cat, jacket,* or *phone*.

Variation 1: *my, your, his, her*

1. Put a small table or chair in the center of the room. Then have three or four students give you something they have brought to class such as a pencil or a chocolate bar. Try not to let others see who gave you what. Then set the objects down on the table (or chair).
2. Have students stand up and form a circle around the table.
3. Model the activity: Pick up an item (e.g. a pen) and say, *This is his pen.* Hand it to someone who is not the owner. Direct that person to say, *It's not my pen. It's her pen,* or *It's your pen.* Direct them to give it to someone else in the circle. Continue until the pen finds its owner.
4. Play a round with the next item but with less direction. Continue until you have practiced with all the items.

Variation 2: *Positive or negative ownership*

1. Have students work in groups to develop a small sketch in which all the members are arguing over ownership of an idea.

They can decide whether the members want credit for a good idea, or they may want to defer blame to someone else for a bad idea, e.g., *It wasn't myyy idea. It was youuur idea!* Here are some possibilities that could go either way:

- Siblings arguing about whose idea it was to buy a beach house together.
- Employees arguing about whose idea it was to allow people to bring dogs to work.
- Friends arguing about whose idea it was to go camping.

2. Have groups perform their sketch, and the audience tries to guess whether people want credit for the idea or whether they are trying to defer blame.

39. Prepositional phrases of time & location

THE GRAMMAR: The prepositions *at*, *in*, and *on* can combine with certain nouns to make prepositional phrases of time and location.

Prepositional phrases of time include:
- *at* + clock times/specific times of day
- *in* + months/years/seasons/periods of time during the day
- *on* + days of the week/dates/holidays

Prepositional phrases of location include:
- *at* + specific places in space (e.g. *at home, at the bus stop*)
- *in* + towns/cities/countries
- *on* + roads/rivers & surfaces (e.g. *on my desk, on the floor*)

Aim: Students race to identify prepositions that correctly complete statements of time and location.

Level: Beginner (A1)

Preparation: 15-20 sentences that use the prepositions *in*, *on*, and *at* for time or location (see below); two flyswatters or rolled-up pieces of paper to "slap" the prepositions on the board

Time: 10 minutes +

Activity

1. Review prepositions in, on, and at, for time and location by putting places and dates on the board and having pairs or groups try to decide which preposition goes before each. (See below)

2. Clear the board. Write the prepositions *in, on,* and *at* several times in multiple places on the board.

3. Divide the class into two teams. Bring a student from each team up to the board and give each a flyswatter (or a comparable slapping object, such as a rolled-up piece of paper).

4. Tell students they must slap the preposition that is missing in each sentence you read and then repeat the sentence with the correct preposition. Read your sentences with the word "blank" in place of the preposition:

    - I went to bed [at] midnight. Read *I went to bed blank midnight.*
    - There were not many people [on] the bus.
    - She lives [in] the United States.
    - My phone is [on] the desk.
    - I like to exercise [in] the mornings.
    - We walked [on] the sidewalk.
    - They waited [at] the bus stop for an hour.
    - The train leaves [at] noon.
    - There is a bank [on] the corner of the street.
    - Do you like living [in] Chicago?
    - The pool is closed [in] the winter.
    - My job interview is [on] April 26.
    - I took a nap [in] the afternoon.
    - Angie is still [at] home.
    - There's cake [in] the fridge.

5. The first student to slap a preposition must say the preposition s/he chose and repeat the sentence with that preposition. If the preposition and sentence are correct, give his/her team a point. If the student is incorrect, allow the other player to slap and shout out the preposition, and say the sentence with the preposition. Give his/her team a point if the preposition and sentence are correct.

6. Continue until all students have had a chance to come up to the board. The team with the most points wins the game.

Variation

For lower-level classes, focus only on prepositions of location (e.g. *in class, on the subway, at home*) or prepositions of time (e.g. *at noon, on Saturday, in the evenings*, etc.)

40. Present perfect for recent actions

THE GRAMMAR: The present perfect is formed with *has/have* + the past participle (*-d, -t, -(e)n*). It can be used to refer to past events that affect the present.
- I've lost my glasses, so I am not able to read.
- He's cut his hand, so he needs a bandage.
- We've paid the bill, so we can leave.

Aim: Students use the present perfect to describe live actions
Level: Low-intermediate (A2-B1)
Preparation: A list of cues to act out written on cards (see below)
Time: 15 minutes +

Activity

1. Review the present perfect forms and give examples of situations where it has an effect on the present. Then model the activity. For example, your cue might be, "I've run out of gas, so I

Activities

can't drive." Pretend to be driving and run out of gas. Get out of your "car" and continue the mime. Then break out of your role, turn to the class and say, "What's wrong?" to elicit, "You've run out of gas." Elicit or introduce other contexts where the immediate past affects the present. For example,

- *I'm not hungry because I've just eaten.*
- *I'm tired because I've just run a marathon.*

2. Have a volunteer pick up a cue card from the list below and model the activity. Other students should guess using the present perfect. Then another student takes a turn. (If your class is big, you might want to have them do it in two or three groups.)

    - I've been in the sun too long, and I've gotten a sunburn.
    - I've eaten too much and I've gotten sick.
    - I'm late, so I've missed the bus.
    - I've lost my wallet, so I can't pay for my groceries.
    - I've locked myself out of my car/house.
    - I've just gotten a great/terrible grade on a test.
    - My phone has run out of battery, so I dropped my call.
    - I've just seen my ex-boyfriend/girlfriend, and I don't want her/him to see me.
    - I've just eaten something that tastes terrible/delicious.
    - I've just scored a goal!

Variation

Have students work in teams to create a tableau for other teams to guess. Each group gets a few minutes to plan and figure out their body language and expression. Encourage them to use the floor as well as standing and sitting for dramatic effect. Then have them come out and when you say "Freeze!", the team members all get into position. Others must guess the situation using the present perfect. Below are some ideas for situations:

- An alien ship has just appeared in the sky.
- You've been offered cabbage soup for dinner.
- You've just seen an athlete score a goal. (Suggestion: Some of you might be happy, others upset.)
- Tourists have just arrived at the Great Wall of China.
- A robber has just pulled out a gun and wants your money and jewelry.

41. Present perfect with *ever* and *never*.

> **THE GRAMMAR:** *Ever* is used with the present perfect to ask questions. *Never* is used for a negative response. When the response is affirmative, use a number or adverb of frequency.
> - Have you ever gone to the opera?
> - No, I've never been.
> - Oh, I've been many times. I like it.

Aim: Students practice asking and answering questions with present perfect and ever/never.

Level: Intermediate (B1)

Preparation: One blank slip of paper for each student

Time: 15 minutes +

Activity

1. Review questions, responses, and negative responses with present perfect and ever/never. You can do this by having students unscramble sentences on the board. Then discuss the patterns. Use the example below or create your own.

    A: ghost seen Have ever a you?
    B: have I No, seen a never ghost.
    A: were I movies have many seen ghosts, they in but the.

2. Pass out a blank slip of paper to each student and have them

write one thing they have done that no one knows about. They should write clearly. They should NOT write their name.

3. Collect the slips and then redistribute them randomly.

4. Have students read their paper and turn the statement into a "Have you ever . . .?" question.

5. Have everyone stand up, walk around, and ask the question until they find the person who has done the action on their slip. They should practice responding, "I have never . . ." if the slip isn't theirs. Also tell them to say, "Yes, but that's not me!" if the slip is true of them, but they didn't write it.

6. As they mingle, walk around and notice any errors to clarify later. They may try to use a double negative with never, for example.

42. Present perfect progressive

> **THE GRAMMAR** The present perfect progressive is formed by *has/have been* + verb + *-ing*. It is used to describe ongoing recent events that have impacted or explain one's current state.
> - I have been running. (so I'm hot and sweaty)
> - She has been traveling. (so she is tired)
> - We have been crying. (so our eyes are red)

Aim: Students use the present perfect progressive to describe an experience that affects their current state.

Level: Intermediate to High-intermediate (B1-B2)

Preparation: None

Time: 15 minutes +

Activity

1. Review the present perfect progressive and its form. Make sure students also know the meaning of predator and prey. They

should also know some examples of each, such as a bear, a tiger, a hunter, a monster, a deer, a rabbit, a camper.

2. Clear an open space in the room. Divide the class in half. Have the first half come to the front of the room and walk around and fill the space. Then say, "Now you are a forest. You must become trees and freeze." Encourage them to use their arms and bodies to look like trees.

3. Have the second half come to the front. Tell them they are prey and they are trying to escape from an imaginary predator. Have them move around the "forest" as if they were being chased. Let this continue for 60 – 90 seconds. Then call "Freeze!" again.

4. Now ask the prey to stand on one side. Interview the "prey" by asking present perfect progressive questions and directing students to answer in complete sentences:
   - What have you been doing?
   - Why have you been doing that?
   - Where have you been hiding?
   - How long have you been running?

   Ask other follow-up questions to elicit the form/forms. They can say what they've been escaping from and what they've been doing or even how long they've been doing it to build a "narrative," depending on their creativity.

5. Have them switch roles. This time the former "prey" walk around and fill the room to become trees. Call "Freeze!", and the former trees become predators. Have them move around as if they were hunting/chasing the prey. Again give 60 – 90 seconds. Call "Freeze!" And ask present perfect progressive questions.
   - What have you been doing?
   - Why have you been doing that?
   - Where have you been looking?
   - How long have you been hunting?

6. (Optional) Have students write a short description of the event using the present perfect progressive.

Variation

Consider having prey and predators in the same scenario for added excitement. You can also change the context. Make it a jungle or a busy train station with a cops-and-robbers theme. In the latter case, the "set" can become walls or kiosks that the predator and prey have to navigate.

43. Present progressive

THE GRAMMAR: The present progressive is used to describe actions that are happening right now or are currently in progress. It is formed with *am/is/are* + verb + *-ing*. In spoken English, we often use contractions with the subject and the verb *be*.
- I'm driving to work.
- Right now, he's talking on the phone.
- I can't believe it's snowing outside!
- They're doing construction on the highway.

Aim: Students use the present progressive to describe live actions
Level: Beginner to Intermediate (A1-B1)
Preparation: A list of activities and chores people do in specific locations that can be easily acted out (see below).
Time: 15 minutes +

Activity

1. Review the present progressive and provide or elicit some examples of chores or activities that happen at specific places (see below). For lower-level students, consider listing them on the board for reference.
2. Divide the class in half or thirds by numbering them off. Have the first set come to the front. Choose a context. Then secretly

tell one student to act out doing an activity from that context. For example, you could start with the gardening list and have Student A start digging a hole.

In the garden	In the kitchen	At an airport	In the park
digging a hole mowing the lawn watering the grass picking flowers	washing the dishes cooking soup chopping vegetables	pulling a suitcase going through security saying goodbye	playing Frisbee riding a bike grilling barbecue exercising

While Student A acts out digging a hole, elicit a present progressive description from the class e.g., "She is digging a hole." Then invite Student B to Join A and mime an additional action. Again elicit the form from the seated students. Continue with additional students, having them think up their own progressive actions. Continue to point out that this is happening right now. Keep the actors doing the activity and finish by eliciting the plural form. What are they all doing? E.g., "They are working in the garden."

(Optional) Have students ask each other questions to practice the question form, e.g., "What is Ninoska doing?"

3. Continue with the next sets to provide plenty of practice and set the idea that this structure is a temporary thing happening right now.

Variation

For higher levels, clarify the difference between present progressive and gerunds. Have them sit after each "performance" and talk about how they "feel" about the activities. You can provide stems such as:

| I enjoy | washing the dishes |

I like	watering the grass
I hate	going through security
I don't like	folding laundry

Point out that in sharing feelings about an activity, the verbs are *enjoy, like, hate,* and *don't like*, not the *-ing* form. This illustrates the concept of gerunds as nouns.

44. Present simple affirmative

> **THE GRAMMAR:** The present simple is often used to share factual information and habits. It is formed with the subject plus base form of the verb, except in the third person singular (*he, she, it*). In this case, the verb is followed by -s.
> - I play the piano.
> - She sings.
> - Joe books the shows.
> - We practice every weekend.

Aim: Students act out and narrate a variety of present simple statements in the third person singular

Level: Beginner to Intermediate (A1-B1)

Preparation: None

Time: 15 minutes +

Activity

1. Review the features of the present simple with a focus on third person -s. You can do this by writing a sentence and ask students to change the subject to he or she, and to point out the third person -s.

I wear boots to class.	He wears boots to class.
We sing in the shower.	She sings in the shower.
They catch frogs.	It catches frogs.

2. Introduce the activity by saying the frame below, but instead of saying the verbs, act them out.

   I _____ (sleep) all day, and I _____ (watch TV) all night.

3. Prompt a volunteer to say the sentence about you in the third person. For example,

   The student might say, "The teacher sleeps all day, and watches TV all night." Draw attention to the correct or missing third person -s on the verb. For beginners, elicit a list of verbs that are part of people's daily routines that students can draw from for the activity.

4. Have the students stand in a circle so everyone can see everyone else. Then start the activity. Student A says the frame but acts out the verbs, e.g. *clean/eat* would be *I ____ all day, and I ____ all night.* Then ask Student B to say the complete sentence using A's name and the third person -s in the statement, *Keiko cleans all day and eats all night.* Then have Student B repeat the frame while acting out a new pair of verbs, and have Student C say the sentence.

5. Gently refocus their attention if they forget the -s and make sure they repeat the sentence correctly before moving on to the next person.

6. Continue the activity until all the students have had a chance to act out and repeat the form in the frame.

Variation

Have a student act out their actual daily routine. Then have students in pairs tell each other what the person does, paying attention to the form.

45. Present simple with *some* & *any*

THE GRAMMAR: *Some* is used with plural count and non-count nouns in questions and statements. *Any* is used in negative statements and sometimes questions.
- Do you want some flowers?
- Does she have some advice?
- Do we need any gas?
- I don't want any flowers.
- He doesn't expect any gifts.
- They don't own any tools.

Aim: Students practice offering items and accepting or refusing the offer

Level: High-beginner (A2)

Preparation: None

Time: 15 minutes +

Activity

1. Review the patterns for the present simple with the verb *want*. For example, you can ask student A, "Do you want a sandwich," and then have Student A ask Student B a different "Do you want . . ." question. Go around the room, and then have them try to remember who wants what and make a list of sentences with third person -s on the board. Make some of them plural and clarify patterns as needed.

2. Have students brainstorm a vocab list of things that neighbors might have in their home, garage, or kitchen that they might want to get rid of. List some that are potentially desirable and some that are not. Write the list on the board for students to refer back to. An example list is on the following page.

snow boots	beach towels	oranges
pots	paper bags	potatoes
a shovel	a child's bicycle	a kitten
some light bulbs	some cardboard boxes	sugar
wood	doorknobs	videos
some children's shoes	coffee mugs	tea
pillows	socks	yellow paint

3. Warm up by nominating and asking students random questions with the form and eliciting full answers such as the following:
   - Do you want some money? Yes, I want some money.
   - Do you want some yellow paint? No, thanks, I don't want any yellow paint.

4. Have students stand in a circle. Then tell them you are going to offer something to Student A, and A may accept it or refuse. Model by pretending to hold something, e.g., some snow boots, and saying to Student A, "Do you want some snow boots?" Student A can accept by saying, "Oh yes, I really want some snow boots!" and mime accepting them. Then they continue by offering the snow boots to someone else in the circle.

5. If A says, "No thank you. I don't want any snow boots," go to a second person and offer your snow boots (or a new item). Continue until you have a taker who then continues the chain.

6. Encourage students to use their voice and body language to communicate enthusiasm or a decisive "No!"

7. Listen for errors to give feedback in the moment or after the activity.

46. Present simple with negative forms

THE GRAMMAR: *Do not* + verb is used with *I*, *you*, *we* and *they*. *Does not* is used with *he*, *she*, and *it*. Both are used to create a negative simple present statement.
- I do not like milk.
- She does not own a car.
- We do not have daughters.
- It does not work.

The contractions are *don't* and *doesn't*.

Aim: Students use simple negative to practice making excuses
Level: Beginner (A1)
Preparation: Imaginary scenarios (see below)
Time: 20 minutes

Activity

1. Review the forms for past simple. You can have students ask you questions, and you can respond in the negative. Then have volunteers write your exact words on the board. This helps you check what they heard. You can also divide the class in half and direct the left side to ask the right side a question, such as "Do you have a blue cat?" The right side should respond, "No, I don't have a blue cat." Switch to continue the drill. You can also nominate individuals to answer questions about a singular third student, e.g., "Does Walter have orange hair?" to elicit "doesn't."

2. Have students stand in a circle with one student in the middle. That student has an imaginary box of kittens to give away. Tell all the students to think about as many reasons as they can to refuse the kitten. Tell the student they have to try to give away a kitten by convincing people in the circle to take one.

3. The student with the kittens then nominates someone in the circle and tries to convince them to take a kitten. That person has to try not to take the kitten by giving an excuse. There is a rule. They can use *don't* ("I don't like cats") or *doesn't* ("My apartment manager doesn't allow cats"), but if they say *I can't*, then they have to take a kitten and become the person in the middle. (You could also use the word *sorry*, as it is another word that usually comes out when we make excuses.)
4. Continue the game substituting other favors and other players. Optional: Listen for errors to deal with at a feedback section at the end.

47. Pronouns (subject)

THE GRAMMAR: Subject pronouns are used to refer back to a noun that has been previously introduced. *He, she, it*, and *they* are the most commonly used subject pronouns.
- My brother Paul works as a mechanic. He likes working on cars.
- My mother is a very caring person. She calls me every night to ask how I'm doing.
- That car is expensive. It costs over $30,000.
- Her parents live in Cambodia. They own a rice farm.

Aim: Students listen to sentences and identify the correct subject pronoun by slapping it on the board

Level: Beginner (A1)

Preparation: Two fly swatters or rolled-up pieces of paper; a set of statements with subject pronouns

Time: 15 minutes +

Activity

1. Review by writing the pronouns *he, she, it*, and *they* on the board. Ask: *Which pronoun is used for a man? Which is used*

Activities

for a woman? Which pronoun is used for several men or several women? Which pronouns do we use for things or objects? Which one is singular? Which one is plural?

2. On the board, draw four large boxes. Label the boxes: *He, She, It,* and *They*.
3. Divide the class into two teams. Bring a student from each team up to the board and give each a flyswatter (or a comparable slapping object, such as a rolled-up piece of paper).
4. Tell students they must listen to the sentence you read and slap the pronoun referent that correctly refers back to the subject of the sentence. Read the sentence. Use the example sentences below or create your own.
   - My father works as an airline pilot. *(He)*
   - The students weren't happy about all the homework. *(They)*
   - My sister recently moved to Japan. *(She)*
   - The school cafeteria is closed on Fridays. *(It)*
   - Her brothers live in different countries. *(They)*
   - The bus was late this morning. *(It)*
   - My brother studies engineering. *(He)*
   - The woman felt embarrassed. *(She)*
   - Men in my country like to watch soccer. *(They)*
   - The rain was bad this morning. *(It)*
5. Give a point to the student who slaps the correct pronoun box first. Continue until all students have had a chance to come up to the board. The team with the most points wins the game.

Expansion

Ask students to take out a piece of paper. Dictate 5-8 of the sentences and have students copy them down, leaving space between each one. Repeat as necessary. Then ask students to write another sentence after each sentence that uses a pronoun and gives a supporting detail about the main sentence, e.g. *My father works as an airline pilot. <u>He flies about 60 hours per week</u>.*

48. Quantifiers with food

THE GRAMMAR: Food quantifiers are phrases we use to measure different amounts of food. They can be used before count and noncount nouns.
- a slice of bread
- a bag of chips
- a bottle of milk
- a bowl of rice

Aim: Students practice phrases with food quantifiers
Level: Beginner to High-beginner (A1-A2)
Preparation: A ball or beanbag
Time: 5 minutes +

1. Review or introduce common quantifiers of food and write them on the board as shown below. Elicit the kinds of foods we can use after each quantifier, e.g. *a jar of pickles, a bowl of soup, a bag of flour,* etc. Keep the list of quantifiers on the board for students to refer to during the game.

a bar of	a bowl of	a can of	a jar of	a piece of
a bag of	a box of	a carton of	a glass of	a slice of
a bottle of	a bunch of	a cup of	a loaf of	a kilo/ pound of

2. Explain the game to the students. The student with the ball, Student A, will randomly pick a food quantifier from the board. When she says the quantifier, she will throw the ball to another student in the circle, and Student B will complete the phrase with an appropriate food. For example, Student A says, "a glass of…" and Student B says "Milk, a glass of milk." Student B then chooses a new quantifier and throws it to Student C, and so on.

Activities

3. Have students stand in a circle. (For larger classes, form two circles). Show them the ball or the beanbag. Model the activity first, saying a food quantifier from the board and throwing the ball to one of the students to complete the phrase with a food item. Offer help as necessary.
4. Set a timer for 5 minutes and start the ball toss. Monitor to make sure all students have had a chance or two to complete a phrase.

Variation

To make the game more competitive, play it as an elimination game. If a student cannot immediately come up with a food to complete the phrase (after 1-2 seconds), she must leave the circle. Alternatively, if a student does not use the plural form of a noncount noun, e.g. *a jar of pickles*, she is eliminated. Continue the game until you have one person standing to declare a winner.

49. Restrictive and nonrestrictive clauses

THE GRAMMAR: Restrictive and nonrestrictive clauses are two types of adjective clauses that follow nouns. They are often found between subjects and verbs. Restrictive clauses identify which subject one is referring to, whereas nonrestrictive clauses give "extra information" about the subject. Because nonrestrictive clauses are not essential, they are set off from the subject and main verb with commas.

- Children who play group sports learn about teamwork. (restrictive)
- The dress that she bought online never arrived. (restrictive)
- My mother, who lives in England, has lived in the same town for 80 years. (nonrestrictive)
- Sydney, which is home to over 4 million, is Australia's largest city. (nonrestrictive)

Aim: Students recognize restrictive and nonrestrictive clauses in speech

Level: High-Intermediate to Advanced (B2-C1)

Preparation: A set of statements with restrictive and nonrestrictive clauses (see below)

Time: 15 minutes +

Activity

1. Review the structure. For example, you can write two sentences: one with a restrictive clause between the subject and verb, and one with a nonrestrictive clause. Do not add any commas. An example might be: *The person who wrote the novel is from Argentina. César Aira (,) who is Argentinian (,) is a famous novelist.* Ask for volunteers to read each sentence. Then review which sentence requires commas and why and add them to the sentence.

2. Explain that when speaking, we pause before and after nonrestrictive clause to indicate that the information is less important than the information in the main clause. Model this physically. Read the example sentence with the nonrestrictive clause. Squat down when you read the clause so that your body drops down during the clause and comes back up after the clause.

3. Have students stand up and form groups of three. Tell the members in the group to stand side-by-side. Their order (left-to-right) will represent the order of the sentences they hear: the subject, the (non)restrictive clause, and the verb/predicate.

4. Explain that you will read sentences with restrictive and nonrestrictive clauses. Students will follow these rules:
    a. If students hear a restrictive clause, they should all give a "thumps up" to indicate that the clause is not set off from the rest of the sentence.

Activities

b. If the students hear a nonrestrictive clause, the middle student should give a "thumbs down" to show that the information in the clause is not necessary, while the other two students (representing the subject and predicate) give a "thumbs up" to indicate the main sentence.

5. Read 8-10 sentences with restrictive and nonrestrictive clauses. After reading 3-4 sentences, yell "Switch!" so that there is a different student standing in the middle. Use the sentences below or your own. Make each group of 3-4 sentences similar in context.

    - The test <u>that we took last week</u> was difficult. (restrictive)
    - Claudia, <u>who I study with on weekends</u>, passed the test. (nonrestrictive)
    - Dominic, <u>who is also a good student</u>, failed the test. (nonrestrictive)
    - The students <u>who failed the test</u> can take it again next week. (restrictive)
    - The man <u>who caused the accident</u> was texting on his phone. (restrictive)
    - His car, <u>which was only a few days old</u>, was completely destroyed. (nonrestrictive)
    - The other driver, <u>who was riding a motorcycle</u>, was taken to the hospital. (nonrestrictive)
    - The people <u>who saw the accident</u> gave a report to the police. (restrictive)
    - The Louvre, <u>which is located in Paris</u>, is home to the Mona Lisa. (nonrestrictive)
    - The paintings <u>that hang on the walls of the museum</u> are very valuable. (restrictive)
    - Tourists <u>who visit the Louvre</u> can spend a whole day there and will still not see everything. (restrictive)

- King Francis I, who reigned France during the 16th century, opened the Louvre to show off all his art. (non-restrictive)

50. So & such

THE GRAMMAR: *So* and *such* can be used for emphasis. A conventional usage is to pair them with a consequence: *so* + adjective + *that* + a consequence, and *such* + article + adjective + noun + *that* + a consequence. In conversation, we sometimes drop *that*.
- The movie was so bad that I walked out halfway through.
- It was so hot that I burned my tongue.
- It was such a long drive that we didn't arrive until three o'clock in the morning.
- It was such a boring meeting that Esmé fell asleep.

Aim: Students practice using their voices to show emphasis with *so* and *such*

Level: Low-Intermediate (A2-B1)

Preparation: None

Time: 15-20 minutes

Activity

1. Review the meanings of *so* and *such* by playing two parts in a role-play. Emphasize and exaggerate *so* and *such*.

    A: It was a really bad movie.
    B: How bad was it?
    A: It was so bad that we left in the middle.

2. Next, have students take the B role and give another example. Drill the short dialog to help students internalize the intonation.

    A: Teacher: The food was very expensive.

B: Students: How expensive was it?

A: Teacher: It was so expensive that my credit card was declined.

3. Have students stand in a circle. Then start a chain of exaggeration by saying, "My meal was so bad that I didn't finish it." Instruct the person to your left to repeat by try to come up with something worse, such as, "That meal was so bad that I had to leave the table." And the next person continues as in, "That meal was so bad that I threw up!" When a student can't come up with something worse, then start the next student with a new context from the examples below or your own.

- a noisy concert
- a dirty house
- terrible traffic
- a bad driver
- boring meeting
- a great band
- a terrific meal
- a cute puppy or kitten
- a nice beach
- a fun party

4. Continue the chain, giving corrections as needed until everyone has had a turn. Then repeat with *such*, e.g. *That was such a noisy concert that I couldn't hear the band.* Remind students of the slightly different structure and give other feedback as needed.

Variation

Turn the activity into a competition. If a person cannot exaggerate beyond the previous speaker, they must sit down. The last person standing gets the exaggeration award.

51. Stative verbs

THE GRAMMAR: Stative verbs are non-action verbs that are used to describe unchanging situations, express emotions, show possession, and describe the senses. Some stative verbs, such as *know, hate*, and *own* are never used in the progressive (*BE + -ing*). Other stative verbs can have both a stative (non-action) meaning and an active meaning. We can use the progressive when the meaning is active.
- I have two brothers and a sister. (stative - ownership)
- We're having a test today. (active - "taking")
- The soup tastes a little too salty. (stative - senses)
- The chef is tasting the dish to see if it's ready. (active - "eating")

Aim: Students practice listening and responding to stative and dynamic verbs

Level: High-beginner to Intermediate (A2-B1)

Preparation: A list of sentences with stative and action verbs in context (see below)

Time: 5 minutes +

Activity

1. Review stative verbs that can change meaning and be active ("dynamic"). Verbs that can have both a stative and active meaning include: *be, have, look, see, smell, sound, taste, think,* and *weigh*. If necessary, write example sentences on the board to review the two different meanings, e.g. *I have a really bad headache.* (stative) *vs. Fatima is having a party at her house.* (active - "hosting").'

2. Ask students to form a circle and walk in a clockwise direction. Tell students they will hear sentences with stative and active verbs. If the verb has a stative meaning, they must stop walking

to illustrate that it is not an action. If the verb has an active meaning, they must walk (or continue to walk) to emphasize that it is an action.

3. Read a list of 10 or more sentences with verbs used with stative and active meanings, using a random order. Use the examples below or create your own.

   - It smells like there's something rotten in the fridge. (stop)
   - I'm smelling something that reminds me of my childhood. (walk)
   - That sounds like a good plan. Let's do it! (stop)
   - The school is sounding the fire alarm. We must leave the building. (walk)
   - Do you have a pen I can borrow? (stop)
   - He's having a hard time in his algebra class. (walk)
   - My cat weighs more than my chihuahua. (stop)
   - I'm weighing the potatoes to see how much they'll cost. (walk)
   - My parents think that I should major in accounting. (stop)
   - What are you thinking about right now? (walk)
   - My house is close to a nice park.
   - Please stop – you're being very rude! (walk)

52. Superlatives

THE GRAMMAR: The superlative is used to make comparisons among groups of three or more people, items, or characteristics. All superlative forms use the article *the*. One-syllable adjectives and two-syllable adjectives ending in *-y* add *-est* to the adjective (and the *y* becomes *i*). Longer adjectives use *least/most* + the base form of the adjective. With nouns, we use *most, least* (noncount), and *fewer* (count).
- Jamie is the tallest person in the room.
- He is the messiest person I know.
- This is the most difficult question to answer.
- That's the least possible explanation.
- Who has the most money?
- She has the fewest problems.

Aim: Students line up according to categories using superlative adjectives and nouns

Level: Intermediate (B1)

Preparation: None

Time: 15 minutes +

Activity

1. Review the forms of superlative adjectives and nouns. A fun way to do this is with pictures of aliens that go from cute to intelligent to scary. Alien A is the cutest. Alien B is the most intelligent. Alien C is the scariest! Practice the different forms and review the way the number of syllables affects the pattern. Remind students that we use *the least* with noncount nouns and *the fewest* with count nouns.

2. Divide the class groups so you have teams of 5–7 students. Tell students that they must arrange themselves in correct ascending or descending order depending on the adjectives and

nouns you use. The first team to be in the correct order wins the round.

3. Use the following categories (or your own). Tell the students to line up:
   a. From the tallest to the shortest
   b. From the youngest to the oldest
   c. From the least talkative to the most talkative
   d. From the longest hair to the shortest hair
   e. From the quietest to the loudest
   f. From owning the cheapest shoes to owning the most expensive shoes
   g. From owning the most shoes to owning the fewest shoes
   h. From having the most siblings to having the fewest siblings

4. Give each team a point for being in the correct order. Confirm the order by observations (e.g. who has the longest hair) or by asking the students questions (e.g. "When were you born?" "How much did your shoes cost?" etc.)

Variation

Review and contrast comparatives and superlatives by having one of the groups form a pyramid in which the tallest student stands front and center, the middle height students crouch in front of the tallest student, and the shortest students form a row sitting on the floor in front. Elicit comparative and superlative examples from the class to review. Have each group take a turn organizing themselves into a pyramid with alternative themes such as age or how busy they are.

53. Tag questions

> **THE GRAMMAR:** Tag questions are added at the end of a statement to confirm an assumption or expectation, and sometimes to anticipate agreement. They consist of a helping verb (*be, have, do*) and a subject. Pronunciation is an important element in showing whether someone is genuinely inquiring or inviting the other person to agree with them about something.
> - These biscuits are good, aren't they?
> - You were there, weren't you?
> - He hasn't fixed it yet, has he?
> - You told the truth, didn't you?

Aim: Students practice choosing the right tag question in different tenses in a competition

Level: High-beginner to Intermediate (A2-B1)

Preparation: Two identical sets of tags that correspond to a prepared list of sentences (see below)

Time: 10 minutes +

Activity

1. Review tag questions in the tenses that you want to focus on. A matching activity is often useful for this.

2. Have students notice how the affirmative sentences need a negative tag and vice versa. One way to do this is by saying the first part of a sentence and eliciting the tag from students. You can also create a chart on the board.

3. Divide the class into two teams. Then give each member of the team a slip of paper with a different tag. Give them a place to stand with no obstacles to the board. Tell them to think about what kind of sentence the tag will follow so they know what to listen for.

Activities

TEAM A	TEAM B
isn't it?	isn't it?
don't we?	don't we?
doesn't she?	doesn't she?
is he?	is he?
haven't they?	haven't they?
are you?	are you?
don't they?	don't they?
will we?	will we?
doesn't it?	doesn't it?
didn't he?	didn't he?
hasn't she?	hasn't she?
isn't there	isn't there

4. Tell students you will say a sentence, and whoever has the right tag must come to the board and hold up their tag. The first person to the board will get a point for their team. If they have the wrong tag, they lose a point. Try a few practice runs. Use the sentences below or create your own.

- It's a spider . . .
- We need milk . . .
- She looks good . . .
- He's not here . . .
- They've left . . .
- You're not ready, . . .
- They want one . . .
- We won't drive . . .
- It has a fireplace . . .
- He wrecked the car . . .
- She's bought the house . . .
- There's water.

- It's raining . . .
- We have time . . .
- She works downtown . . .
- He's a doctor.
- They've seen us.
- You're tried . . .
- They live next to you . . .
- We won't get lost . . .
- It gets cold a lot . . .
- He got fired . . .
- She's been outside . . .
- There's another one . . .

5. Start the game and tally points. To make it more student-centered, give the sentences to one of the students to read out loud.

Expansion

1. Work on the pronunciation aspect of tag questions by having students use their voice. After they've matched some sentences and tags, have them practice falling intonation to show they are certain, and rising intonation to show they are uncertain. Put them in pairs and have them read the sentences with tags aloud and have the partner guess whether they are sure or not sure.
2. Have students use the cues to create and perform short dialogs. Tell them to decide who they are, where they are, and how they feel.

54. *There is/There are* with prepositional phrases

THE GRAMMAR: At basic levels, we use *there is/there are* to introduce a noun + a prepositional phrase to indicate where something is located.
- There's some trash on the ground.
- There's a parking spot over there.
- There are birds in the sky.
- There are tigers in the forest.

Aim: Students respond to imaginary features in the environment as they go on an imaginary walk across the city
Level: Beginner (A1)
Preparation: None
Time: 10 minutes +

1. Review *There is/There are* by eliciting examples with a picture or items in the classroom so students are clear about the language

being practiced. For very low levels, introduce the nouns you will use such as *birds, dogs, trash, an ambulance*, etc.

2. Tell students you are going to take them on a walk and talk about different things you'll "see" They should listen and then respond with happy, nervous, sad, or scared responses/exclamations such as "Ahhh"' "Ohhh" "Uh oh!" or "Oh no!" and physical gestures. You might want to practice or drill these as well.

3. Model by saying *Look, there are some birds in the sky!* Point up and invite the students to respond with an exclamation. Here are some additional examples.
   - There's a squirrel in the tree.
   - There are children in the park.
   - There's a fire in that house!
   - There's a bus with a flat tire over there.
   - There are rats in the street.
   - There are flowers in that garden.

4. Have students stand up and line up behind you. Walk around the classroom, pointing and saying *There is/There are* + nouns, and letting them respond.

5. Nominate a student or volunteer to lead the walk. They should say, *Look, there's a* + singular noun or *There are* + a plural noun, and students should respond. At this point, take notes and provide correction. Continue rotating different students through the line.

Expansion

After the activity, have students sit down and write down two lists, one about positive things in the city, and one about negative things in the city. Have them compare their lists with a partner. Elicit their ideas by having them identify the items they listed using *There is/There are* and write them on the board under the headings "Happy things" and "Unhappy things."

55. This, That, These, Those

> **THE GRAMMAR**: Words such as *this, that, these,* and *those* are often used to show whether an object is near (*this/these*) or far (*that/those*). *These* and *Those* are the plural forms, respectively. Demonstratives can be used on their own as pronouns, or as adjectives describing nouns.
> - This is my cousin, Linda.
> - This soup tastes terrible!
> - These shoes are on sale.
> - Do you see that?
> - I don't like the look of those clouds.
> - Those people are still waiting in line.

Aim: Students demonstrate the meaning of *this/that* and *these/those* through actions

Level: Beginner (A1)

Preparation: A set of statements with *this/that/these/those*

Time: 10 minutes +

Activity

1. Review the uses of demonstrative adjectives and pronouns. Write all four on the board: *this / that / these / those*. Ask students questions to confirm understanding: *Which words are singular? Which are plural? Which ones mean something is close? Which ones mean something is far away?*

2. Ask students to stand in a circle around you. Leave about 3-4 feet between you and the students. Then tell students to listen to the sentences you read and follow these instructions: Step <u>toward</u> you when they hear a sentence with *this* and *these*. Step <u>away from</u> you when they hear a sentence with *that* and *those*. Read 10+ sentences with the various pronouns. Use the ones below or create your own.

Activities

- This is the best meal I've ever had!
- Look at those dark clouds over there!
- That car is going way too fast!
- Can you please put these napkins on the table?
- This computer isn't working.
- These are my new neighbors.
- Is that a train?
- Those people look angry.
- Do you want this last cookie?
- I can't tell what that sound is, can you?

Variations

- Have students also listen for singular and plural. When they hear *this/that*, have them hold up one hand as they move. When they hear *these/those*, have them hold up both hands.
- Give each student a notecard and ask them to write a sentence with *this* or *that* on one side, and *these* or *those* on the other. Use these sentences for the activity.

56. This, That, These, Those II

THE GRAMMAR: *This* refers to nearby single items and non-count nouns. *That* refers to more distant single items and non-count nouns. *These* refers to nearby plural items, and *those* refers to more distant plural items.
- Is this your water bottle (in my hand) yours?
- Do you see that cloud?
- I'll trade you these apples for those crackers.

Aim: Students practice using *this/that* and *these/those* in negotiating a role-play

Level: High-beginner to Low-intermediate (A2-B1)

Preparation: Enough blank squares of paper to give each student five.

Time: 15-20 minutes

Activity

1. Review the meaning and use of *this/that* & *these/those* by modeling distance. It will be relative in terms of what is closer to you or farther away.

2. Pass out five blank squares of paper to each student. Then tell each student to draw one item of the same type of clothing on each square. For example, one student might have five jackets, such as a sports jacket, a windbreaker, a motorcycle jacket, a winter coat, or one can be plaid and another striped. Another student might have five pairs of pants in different styles, each on a separate square.

3. Tell students they are to trade with other students until they have a complete outfit. Give them sentence stems as necessary, such as in the examples below.
   - I'll trade you this shirt for those shoes.
   - I already have a shirt, but I'll trade you these shoes for that hat.
   - Model the activity with several students. Have students practice in front of the class and give feedback as needed. (This is important for making sure the forms are well-established before doing freer practice.)

4. Once you are sure students understand, have them mingle and try to trade until each person has a complete outfit.

Variations

- Practice again using different kinds of items, such as ingredients for a picnic or meal, or tools to build something.

- Set up a simulation of a trading post where different farmers, ranchers, and fishermen try to trade their items for goods. In this case, different groups can come up while others watch, and the teacher can monitor the use of the target grammar.

57. Too & enough

THE GRAMMAR: We use *too* in front of adjectives when they are at an impossible extreme. We use *not enough* for the same meaning to show a deficit.
- It's too hot. I can't pick it up.
- I'm too clumsy. I don't want to enter a dance competition.
- I'm not brave enough. I can't go skydiving.
- It's not hot enough. We need to put it back in the oven.

Aim: Students use emotional intonation to practice using *too* and *enough* to make excuses

Level: High-beginner to Low-Intermediate (A2-B1)

Preparation: None

Time: 20 minutes +

Activity

1. Review the structure by modeling one of the phrases from the box below, eliciting a sentence, and writing it on the board. Discuss the meaning of *too* and *to* in context.
2. Elicit a word bank of adjectives that describe physical characteristics and states such as *tired, short, tall, lazy, weak*, etc.
3. Invite a volunteer to come to the front of the room and give the volunteer impossible instructions. For example, touch the ceiling. The volunteer will not be able to do it, but they should try. Then ask the class, "Why can't Anya touch the ceiling?" to

elicit, "She's too short." If students need a hint, tell them to use the word *too*.

4. Repeat the process with *enough*, by asking, "What's another way to say it?" to elicit, "She's not tall enough." To enhance the kinesthetics, apply gentle pressure on the volunteer by saying something like, "Please! Can't you just try!" or "Just try a little *harder!*" Use your voice and gesture to get them to repeat their excuse with more intonation. You can provide examples of response if you like, such as the ones below. (This may be useful for them in later encounters.)

   - I'm really sorry, but I'm just too…
   - I'd like to help, but I can't. I'm not…enough.

5. Create a support list on the board such as the one on the next page and make sure students know the vocabulary. It's okay if some of them are silly.

6. Have students stand and form two lines face-to-face, Line A and Line B. The first person in Line A (A1) gives the first person in Line B (B1) directions. B1 responds with a sincere and heartfelt apology and makes an excuse using the target language with voice and gesture, and then asks A2 to do something. A2 gives an excuse and asks B2 and so on until all the students have had a turn.

Activities

Instructions	Adjectives for describing self	
Can you please, • touch the ceiling. • pick up that desk and move it. • run a marathon with me. • invite the president to lunch. • climb a tree and take a photo. • eat this chocolate cake. • babysit my children. • help me move to a new apartment. • go stand under that chair. • go ziplining with me.	*I'm sorry . . .* (too) shy weak busy scared lazy full short clumsy tired	(not enough) hungry brave energetic tall graceful
	Adjectives for describing things	
I think you should . . . • buy this sports car. • try on this jacket. • wear these shoes. • eat this soup. • read this book. • take this sweater. • hold this pot. • take advanced math. • walk to Chicago.	*Are you kidding?* (too) expensive far away long big/small cold/hot ugly old hard	(not . . .enough) cheap close short good easy new big/small hot/cold

58. Used to

THE GRAMMAR: We use *used to* + the base form of a verb to talk about habits or situations that were true in the past but are no longer true today.
- I used to ride my bike to school. (I'm no longer in school.)
- I used to work in a restaurant. (Now I work in an office.)
- I used to smoke. (Now I don't smoke.)

Aim: Students practice *used to* in a role-play and reflect on past situations

Level: High-beginner to Low-intermediate (A2-B1)

Preparation: None

Time: 10-20 minutes

Activity

1. Review the structure by introducing a clear context for *used to*. For example, list technology devices such as a mobile phone, a microwave, and a GPS. Have students tell you what they use them for. Ask what people did before these were invented, and invite students to give examples, such as the ones below. Clarify the meaning and form.
    - People used to go home to make phone calls.
    - People used to use cameras.
    - People used to cook everything on a stove.

2. Put students in pairs or groups of three and direct them to create a role-play using the contexts below or create your own. They should use body language, voice and gesture to communicate the situation.
    - Two prisoners in a jail cell talking about their life before prison.

- Two old people in a retirement home talking about their childhood.
- Two rich people enjoying a nice meal in a restaurant.
- Two friends pushing strollers and talking about life before children.
- Two poor people talking about the time when they had money.

3. Give students two minutes to perform for the class. Ask the class to guess what the situation is and whether the people are better off or worse off.

59. *Wh-* questions

THE GRAMMAR: *Wh-* questions (*who, what, when, where, why, how*) practice verb tenses but with a different word order than statements. Questions with *BE* take the order: *Wh-* + *BE* + subject. Questions with verbs other than *BE* follow, *Wh-* + *do/does* + *subject* + *verb*.
- How are you?
- Where is the closest restroom?
- What do you want to do tonight?
- When does the movie end?

Aim: Students prepare a set of questions for a team game
Level: High-beginner (A2)
Preparation: A set of example *Wh-* questions (see below)
Time: 15 minutes +

Activity

1. Review by showing them a selection of the sample questions (see below) and inviting them to create new questions. Then ask which ones they could answer nonverbally.

2. Discuss and elicit volunteers to demonstrate answers through gesture, facial expressions, miming or other sorts of body language, or even draw on the board if they must. Use the examples below or create your own.

    - Who in this class is the most similar to you?
    - Who is your best friend?
    - What is your favorite color?
    - What do you do on the weekends?
    - What is your favorite musical instrument?
    - Where were you born?
    - When do you brush your teeth?

3. Assign students into two teams. Have each team write and edit their own set of *Wh-* questions that could be answered nonverbally. There should be a variety of types, and they should make sure that all the questions are in the correct word order.

4. Explain that the goal is for all questions to be asked and answered in a specified time limit. (Consider the number of students multiplied by two minutes or less.)

5. Have the teams stand in two lines. The first person on each team moves to the front. A person from Team A asks the prepared question, and the person from Team B must answer nonverbally. Set a timer for 90 seconds for the round. If the person from Team A can't guess in time, the answer is given verbally.

6. Next, have a person from Team B ask one of their prepared questions to the next person on Team A. That person has the same time limit to answer nonverbally. Repeat going back and forth across down the row until everyone has had a turn to ask and answer.

7. Check the time to see if they "set a record." You can then play a second round at some point to see if they can beat the record.

Activities

Expansion

Process the activity by going over any errors you noticed. Have a conversation about the way gesture and body language can communicate important messages.

60. Would like

> **THE GRAMMAR:** We use *Would you like* + the base form of the verb to make polite requests and offers. In conversation, we often say *I'd*, the contracted form of *I would*.
>
> We can use *would like/love* + a noun to express a preference for something, and the response *"No, I wouldn't, but..."* to decline an offer.
> - Would you like some cake?
> - I would like a small piece, please.
> - No, I wouldn't, but thank you.
> - I'd love a piece of cake.

Aim: Students practice using *would like* to make a polite offer
Level: Beginner (A1)
Preparation: A list of scenarios (see below)
Time: 15 minutes +

Activity

1. Review the use of *would like* to make and respond to polite requests, and model both the request and the response. Drill the different forms, and practice showing polite intonation.
    - Would you like a cookie?
    - Yes, I'd love a cookie.
    - No. I wouldn't, but thank you for offering!
2. To create a word bank, elicit adjectives that describe objects in the kitchen and around the home such as the following.

hot	cold	heavy	light
magical	beautiful	ugly	slippery
bouncy	enormous	tiny	dirty

3. Have students stand in different places around the room. Show them an imaginary ball by miming a ball in your hands, throwing it and bouncing it. Tell students the ball is sticky, and mime how sticky it is. Then say, "Would you like this sticky ball?" to Student A. Tell Student A to say, "Yes, thank you. I'd love that sticky ball." Or they can say, "No, I wouldn't, but thank you for offering!" If she says yes, throw the imaginary sticky ball to her, and instruct her to say, *Thank you for the sticky ball*. If she says no, try with a new person until someone says yes.

4. Now tell the receiver of the ball that they have a magical power to change the ball into a different kind of ball. It can be hot, cold, wet, dirty, soft, or one of the other adjectives on your list or that the student comes up with. Have Student A offer the ball to a new person (Lenora) and say, *Lenora, would you like this heavy ball?* The student must pretend they have a very heavy ball. Then Lenora says, *Yes thank you, I'd love that heavy ball.* Student A throws it "heavily." Then Lenora catches the heavy ball and says, *Thank you for the heavy ball.* Lenora continues the round by changing the adjective and offering it to another student, repeating the language and miming the adjective.

Expansion

Play another round, but this time allow them to choose to say yes, or they can say, *No, I wouldn't, but thank you for offering!* If the student says no, the thrower must ask a different student.

REFERENCES

Atkinson, D. (2011). 'A sociocognitive approach to second language acquisition: How mind, body, and world work together in learning additional languages.' In D. Atkinson (Ed.), *Alternative approaches to second language acquisition* (pp. 143-166). New York: Routledge.

Gullberg, M. (2008). 'A helping hand? Gesture, L2 learners, and grammar.' In S.G. McCafferty & G. Stam (eds.), *Gesture: Second language acquisition and classroom research* (pp. 185-210). New York: Routledge.

Holme, R. (2009). *Cognitive Linguistics and Second Language Teaching.* Basingstoke: Palgrave Macmillan.

Johnson-Laird, P. N. (1988). *The Computer and the mind: An introduction to cognitive science.* Cambridge, MA: Harvard University Press.

Kelly, L.G. (1969). *25 Centuries of Language Teaching.* Rowley, MA: Newbury House.

Kramsch, C. (2009). *The multilingual subject.* Oxford: Oxford University Press.

Lapaire, J-R. (2005). *La grammaire anglaise en mouvement.* Paris: Hachette.

Lindstromberg, S. and Boers, F. (2005) 'From movement to metaphor with manner-of-movement verbs', *Applied Linguistics,* 26/2.

Long, M.H. & Richards, J.C. (2001). 'Series editors' preface.' In P. Robinson (Ed.) *Cognition and second language instruction.* Cambridge: Cambridge University Press.

Moskowitz, G. (1978). *Caring and sharing in the foreign language class.* Rowley, MA: Newbury House.

Palmer, H.E. (1921). *The principles of language-study.* London: Harrap.

Pinker, S. (1997). *How the mind works.* London: Penguin.

Richards, J.C. & Rodgers, T.S. (2001). *Approaches and methods in language teaching (2nd edition).* Cambridge: Cambridge University Press.

ACTIVITIES BY CEFR LEVEL

A1-A2

A/an before an adjective + noun
A/an/some for first mention & *the* for second mention
Adverbs of frequency
BE verbs in present simple
Comparative adjectives
The zero conditional with the imperative
The first conditional
The future
The future with *will* and *won't*
The imperative
Modals *can* & *can't*
Modals *should* & *shouldn't*
Nouns with quantifiers
Parts of speech
Past simple with yes/no questions
Possessive adjectives
Prepositional phrases of time & location
Present progressive
Wh- questions
Would like

A2-B1

Adverbs of manner
Compound sentences with *and, but & so*
The 2nd conditional
Infinities with the present simple
Nouns count & noncount

Past simple
Past simple and past progressive
Past time clauses with *when* & *while*
Phrasal verbs
Present perfect for recent actions
Present perfect with *ever* and *never*
Present simple affirmative
Present simple with *some* & *any*
Present simple with negative forms
Subject pronouns
Quantifiers with food
So & *such*
Superlatives
Tag questions
There is/There are with prepositional phrases
This, That, These, Those I
This, That, These, Those I
Too & *enough*
Used to

B1-B2

Adjectives with *too*
Infinitives vs. gerunds
Modals past
Noun clauses
Present perfect progressive
Gerunds
Participial adjectives
Participial adjectives past
Participial adjectives present
Passive voice
Passive voice in the past
Past perfect
Stative verbs

Activities by CEFR Level

B2-C1+

Adjective clauses
Passive voice in the past
The 3rd conditional
Restrictive and nonrestrictive clauses

ABOUT THE AUTHORS

ALICE SAVAGE has over 25 years of experience as an author, English language teacher, and teacher trainer. She received her M.A. in TESOL from the School for International Training in Brattleboro, Vermont and currently works as a professor at Lone Star College in Houston, Texas. When not in the classroom, Alice enjoys theater and has written short plays and skits for English learners as well as a book of drama activities and lessons. She also enjoys travel, hiking, and family time.

COLIN WARD received his M.A. in TESOL from the University of London as a US-UK Fulbright Scholar. Today, he is Department Chair and Professor of ESOL at Lone Star College-North Harris in Houston, Texas, USA. He has been teaching ESOL at the community-college level since 2002 and presented at numerous state, national, and international conferences, focusing on topics such as lexical grammar, content-based instruction, and the integration of reading and writing. In his spare time, Colin enjoys spending time with his two daughters, cooking new foods, traveling internationally, and cycling the bayous of Houston.

www.ingramcontent.com/pod-product-compliance
Lightning Source LLC
Chambersburg PA
CBHW030153100526
44592CB00009B/258